VOL. 1

God

MILESTONES

Connecting God's Word to Life

Lifeway Press® Nashville, Tennessee

Student Ministry Publishing

Ben Trueblood
Director, Student Ministry

John Paul Basham
Manager, Student Ministry Publishing

Karen Daniel
Editorial Team Leader

Drew Dixon
Content Editor

Stephanie Livengood
Production Editor

Amy Lyon
Graphic Designer

ISBN: 978-1-5359-6583-5
Item Number: 005816978

Dewey Decimal Classification Number: 204
Subject Heading: RELIGION/ RELIGIOUS
EXPERIENCE, LIFE, AND PRACTICE

Printed in the United States of America.

Student Ministry Publishing
Lifeway Resources
200 Powell Place, Suite 100
Brentwood, TN 37027

We believe that the Bible has God for its author;
salvation for its end; and truth, without any mixture
of error, for its matter and that all Scripture is
totally true and trustworthy. To review Lifeway's
doctrinal guideline, please visit www.lifeway.com/
doctrinalguideline.

Table of
CONTENTS

Milestones was developed by the creators of *Bible Studies for Life: Students*, which exists to point students and student leaders to the application of biblical teaching to everyday life through weekly group Bible studies and additional resources. Every lesson within *Bible Studies for Life* contains a bible study that points students to Jesus, is rooted in Scripture, and provides application for living in today's context. The topics and subjects chosen in each quarter of *Bible Studies for Life* fit within a larger framework called *Levels of Biblical Learning*. *Levels of Biblical Learning* consists of ten theological topics we believe students should grasp before graduating high school. These include:

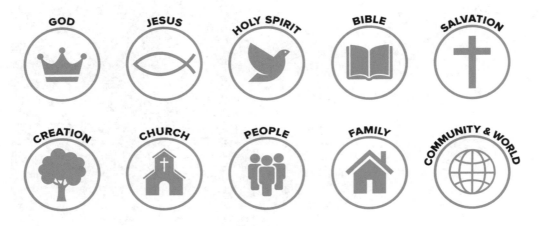

Within these ten topics are 52 theological statements, which make up the core content students would be exposed to and learn each year as they go through *Bible Studies for Life*. The quarterly topics and Scripture passages that make up each lesson in *Bible Studies for Life* are tied the framework of *Levels of Biblical Learning*, which guides the Scripture selection.

While we are able to connect students to the *Levels of Biblical Learning* and the theological statements in each lesson of *Bible Studies for Life*, we wanted to provide a resource capable of going deep into the weight and significance these levels have for personal faith and discipleship. This is what *Milestones* seeks to do. Over the course of six volumes, each of the 52 theological statements will be explored in depth, noting both the theological importance and personal application each has for everyday life. By going through these six volumes, we hope students will grow in their personal knowledge and understanding of God and His world. We also pray that God will use these resources to equip another generation to boldly proclaim the truth of the gospel in a world where Jesus—the truth—is desperately needed.

This Bible-study book includes eight weeks of content for group and personal study. Each session is divided into the following components:

ENGAGE

Each session opens with a *Levels of Biblical Learning Statement*, which gives an overview of the session's topic. Following the statement, each session contains an introduction to help your group as you begin your time together, setting up a natural transition into the material for each week.

DISCUSS

The Discuss section expands upon the *Levels of Biblical Learning Statement*. During this time, groups will explore Scripture, answer questions, and engage with additional content to help explain the session statement.

LIVE IT OUT

The Live It Out section is designed to close out your group time by calling out three specific points of application under the headings of Christ, Community, and Culture. By doing so, this section seeks to demonstrate specifically what the session material teaches us about Christ, how to live in Community, and how to engage with Culture.

DOING, BEING, AND APOLOGETIC STATEMENTS

This section also contains Doing, Being, and Apologetic statements. These statements are directly related to the *Levels of Biblical Learning Statement*, and provide opportunity for the group to expand on what these doctrinal truths communicate about us as individuals, how we are to live, and how we might engage culture apologetically.

DEVOTIONS

Three personal devotions are provided for each session to take students deeper into Scripture and to supplement the content introduced in the group study. With biblical teaching and introspective questions, these sections challenge students to grow in their understanding of God's Word and to respond in faith.

LEADER GUIDE

At the back of this book, you'll find a leader guide to help you prepare each week. This guide will help you gain a broad understanding of the content and learn ways to engage with students throughout your time together.

1

ENGAGE

LEVELS OF BIBLICAL LEARNING STATEMENT
There is one eternal God who reveals Himself to us as Father, Son, and Holy Spirit, and each person of the Trinity has distinct personal attributes.

Think about a person thousands of years ago standing on his land, feeling the wind whipping around his head, watching clouds gather above him, and seeing the beginnings of a tornado form in the distance. All at once, this person, a speck on a tiny patch of an enormous planet is struck with the inescapable feeling:

I am not very big at all.

These kinds of feelings lead us into what it's like to talk about God. He's the biggest, most majestic thing we could ever talk about or pursue. Some of us have grown up in the church talking about Him every week, making Him a staple around our dinner tables or in the music we listen to. Others of us don't know much about Him at all.

Whatever your situation and experience with God, know this: There is not a single thing in this entire universe more all-encompassing, more awe-inspiring than our Creator. And you have a chance to encounter Him.

As we begin this experience of encountering God in His Word, let's build from the ground up. We'll start by exploring one of the most important truths about Him: He is One, and He reveals Himself to us.

Try to think of a few things that "sum you up." It might be activities you are usually involved in, something you're known for, or just places you can usually be found, like the weight room or a dance studio. Describe yourself in one sentence.

DISCUSS

ONE GOD

Every day, Benjamin Franklin would wake up at 5 a.m. and ask himself what good he would do that day before beginning his three hour morning routine. Not everybody has three hours to devote to getting ready, but most of us still have a few things we like to when we wake up.

Are you a morning or night person? What is usually the first thing you do when you wake up? Do you have a morning routine? If so, what does it look like?

When practicing Jews wake up in the morning, the first thing they do is recite the Shema. The Shema comes from Deuteronomy 6, and is one of the most important passages of Scripture for any Jewish man, woman, boy or girl. Read it together out loud:

"Listen, Israel: The LORD our God, the LORD is One."
DEUTERONOMY 6:4

This tells us something incredible: We have one God. There are so many other things that demand our attention, our affection, and our worship, but we have only one thing we're truly devoted to. If this verse were the very first thought that crossed your mind every morning, it would affect the way you go about your day. It would influence the things you consider important. It would color the way you treat people, see yourself and the world around you.

God wanted His people to remember He, alone, is the One deserving of worship and praise and adoration—nothing and no one else is deserving. In Exodus 20:3, He brought the point home by saying, "Do not have other gods besides me."

What are some things in our world today, besides God, that demand our worship?

Why is it so easy to give things that aren't God the worship He deserves?

Our God is one God, and He is the only one worthy of our worship. But He is not some disconnected, distant deity who remains beyond where we can know and understand Him. Instead, He finds it important enough to come to us. We can know Him because He wants to reveal Himself in ways we can understand.

THE TRIUNE GOD   7

GOD REVEALS HIMSELF TO US

Throughout history God has used many ways to show us He's there and to tell us He is knowable. Out loud, read how the writer of Hebrews put it:

> Long ago God spoke to the fathers by the prophets at different times and in different ways. In these last days, he has spoken to us by his Son.
> **HEBREWS 1:1-2a**

A prophet was simply someone who spoke words God told them to speak. The Bible records a lot of prophets' words from Genesis to Revelation. Fortunately for us, they recorded those words so we could continue reading them to this day. Prophecy doesn't necessarily mean someone was predicting the future, but they were speaking the words God told them to say. Speaking through regular people is one way God reveals Himself to us.

But God also used another human to speak to us: Jesus Christ. Jesus was the most unique person to ever live, because He wasn't just a human, He was God's Word in human form. He was totally human, but He was also totally God. Take a look at part of Jesus' prayer just before His arrest:

> "Righteous Father, the world has not known you. However, I have known you, and they have known that you sent me. I made your name known to them and will continue to make it known, so that the love you have loved me with may be in them and I may be in them."
> **JOHN 17:25-26**

Jesus showed His disciples and the entire world who God was by coming to earth and living among them. He taught them the things that God treasures, lived the kind of life they should imitate, and sacrificed Himself so we could understand the kind of love God has for us.

Paul pointed out another way God reveals Himself to us in the Book of Romans.

> For his invisible attributes, that is, his eternal power and divine nature, have been clearly seen since the creation of the world, being understood through what he has made. As a result, people are without excuse.
> **ROMANS 1:20**

God makes Himself known to us through people and through His Son, but He also made Himself known by creating everything we see. He set the world in motion, hung the stars in place, and established the laws that everything in the Universe follows.

Have you ever felt completely in awe of something? How does the Universe reveal God's majesty?

ONE GOD, THREE PERSONS

God's nature is not like anything we can fully understand. As we've seen, our God is one God. We do not have multiple gods we worship, and yet He exists eternally in three distinct persons. We call this the Trinity: the Father, Son, and Holy Spirit. Each of these distinct persons of the godhead have personal attributes.

One of the easiest ways to see this is at the very beginning of everything.

> *In the beginning God created the heavens and the earth. Now the earth was formless and empty, darkness covered the surface of the watery depths, and the Spirit of God was hovering over the surface of the waters. Then God said, "Let there be light," and there was light.*
> **GENESIS 1:1-3**

We can see each member of the Trinity here. We see the Holy Spirit "hovering over the surface" of the waters. We see the Father speaking something in to the darkness. We see His Word going out from His mouth and filling the darkness with light. All three Persons of the Trinity worked together to bring everything in the whole universe to being.

Take a look at this distinction between Father and Son:

> *For us there is one God, the Father. All things are from him, and we exist for him. And there is one Lord, Jesus Christ. All things are through him, and we exist through him.*
> **1 CORINTHIANS 8:6**

- God the Father is the originator of everything we see. He is the uncreated Creator. He is the unmoved Mover. He speaks and things happen.

- His Son is Jesus: the Word of God in human form. He is the official, eternal mouthpiece of all God has ever said.

- God's Spirit is His Power, and Jesus made it available to every one of us—not as something we have to find or call on, but as something that lives inside of us. As Paul said, "Don't you yourselves know that you are God's temple and that the Spirit of God lives in you" (1 Cor. 3:16)?

We have one God who is the Creator of everything who has revealed Himself to us throughout history in hundreds of different ways, showing us He has three distinct Persons: Father, Son, and Holy Spirit. What is most incredible about all of this is that He is still revealing Himself to us today, and we can experience Him as real as ever before.

BEING // All people are created in God's image to reflect Him and live in relationship with Him. Sin damaged that image and brought separation, but Christians are new creations with the distinct privilege of enjoying a restored relationship with God and reflecting His character to the world in a special way.

DOING // Because we are created to reflect God and live in relationship with Him, we should continually pursue God in His Word and through prayer, live in continual fellowship within the church, and help people who do not know Him find Him so they can live in fellowship with Him, too.

APOLOGETIC // Many today believe there are many gods and many ways to heaven, and that we are free to define God according to our personal perspectives. However, Scripture teaches there is one God (Deut. 6:4). The Christian God is different than ones others worship, because He is the Creator of everything, and He actively reveals Himself to us. He wants us to reach out and search for Him. He wants us to listen carefully to what other people are saying and test to see if it is true, because He knows those who seek the truth will find it, and they will find it in Him, because He is the perfect, ultimate source of truth.

CHRIST

The second Person of the Trinity is God the Son. God reveals Himself to us through Jesus. Jesus was not only fully God, but also fully man. He had a physical body, He walked around the same as you and I do, and He experienced the same kinds of temptation we do, except He did it without sinning. He was the only human who ever lived in perfect harmony with the Father.

Can you be a Christian if you don't believe Jesus is God? Why or why not?

COMMUNITY

The Trinity is the perfect model of what community looks like: three persons, one God, all working together for the same purpose. While we are most certainly not part of the Trinity, we can try to model the kind of relationship the Trinity embodies—one where we are completely devoted to one another and work together with other believers for God's glory.

How would you describe your relationship with other believers? What kinds of things do you value?

What things could you do to work together with them to advance God's kingdom?

CULTURE

A large part of our culture doesn't even believe God exists. Some simply don't believe in the God they've heard about, while others just might not think about Him at all. Jesus had something to say about this. He told His disciples, "'By this everyone will know you are my disciples, if you love one another'" (John 13:35).

How can the way we love each other help people see God?

Session 1

DEVOTIONS

ONE GOD

To some it seems arrogant to make an exclusive claim to the truth. As mere humans whose senses are limited and who possess a sin nature, we cannot make the call. We can observe truth through mathematics. We can factually say two and two makes four and doesn't equal "squirrel." However, we lack the authority and even ability to stick a flag in the ground and say, "My personal version of the truth is true and every other version is wrong." However, God can. God is able. He has the authority we lack.

Look at what the Bible says about God's authority to make such claims:

> *Do not have other gods besides me.*
> **EXODUS 20:3**

> *"Listen, Israel: The LORD our God, the LORD is one."*
> **DEUTERONOMY 6:4**

> *For there is one God and one mediator between God and humanity, the man Christ Jesus.*
> **1 TIMOTHY 2:5**

It is not prideful of Him to make the statements He clearly made in these passages. He is the one true God and there is none above Him. So, it is not you as a Christian making this exclusive claim to the truth: it is God Himself. Any objections to this must be taken up with Him. We have no authority on our own, and our own versions of the truth would differ from one to the next. By His authority, God provides the truth and that truth comes to us in a person: Jesus Christ.

Journal here your personal proclamation to God that you believe Him when He rightly claims to be the only God.

GOD REVEALED

You find yourself having been called into existence in a Universe whose Creator is good and who has not hidden Himself. He has revealed Himself in different ways throughout human history. He spoke through prophets of old. He has spoken through His Son. He has given us Scripture. Review how the author of Hebrews explained this:

> *Long ago God spoke to the fathers by the prophets at different times and in different ways. In these last days, he has spoken to us by his Son. God has appointed him heir of all things and made the universe through him.*
> **HEBREWS 1:1-2**

It is clearly understood from everything that has been made that God exists. We can simply observe the Universe and see God's timelessness. We have no excuse (Rom. 1:20). And He didn't leave us in the wilderness to connect vague dots across creation. Instead, He inspired the Bible for us! Look at the way Paul taught Timothy this truth:

> *All Scripture is inspired by God and is profitable for teaching, for rebuking, for correcting, for training in righteousness,*
> **2 TIMOTHY 3:16**

Do you believe all of Scripture is inspired by God? If so, you must feel a sense of urgency to explore all of Scripture. List all the books of the Bible you have read, then compare that list to the whole list of Books in the Bible.

Be brutally honest with yourself. Have you made an effort to get to know God in His Word? Explain.

Create a catalog of how you spend your time. Are there things in your routine you could sacrifice in favor of time in God's Word? If so, journal a commitment to God to prioritize His Word.

TRINITY

Mankind was not created to help God deal with loneliness. Rather, mankind was created out of the overflow of fellowship already present in God the Father, Son, and Holy Spirit. Here's how God Himself described it:

Then God said, "Let us make man in our image, according to our likeness.
GENESIS 1:26a

Have you been drawn by the Holy Spirit to confess that the Son is Lord so you might be reconciled to the Father? This is what happens when someone is saved. We can see the Trinity at work in salvation. Check out what John said about the Trinity's role in salvation.

And we know that the Son of God has come and has given us understanding so that we may know the true one. We are in the true one—that is, in his Son Jesus Christ. He is the true God and eternal life.
1 JOHN 5:20

The idea of the Trinity can be difficult to explain. Theologians with fancy degrees have argued for generations over the best way to illustrate the concept of the Trinity. In fact, skeptics of Christianity may try to use this confusion to make you feel insecure about your faith. However, you likely know more about the Trinity than you realize. If you are able to share the story of how the Holy Spirit convicted you of sin, how you came to confess Jesus as Lord, and you look forward to eternity with the God who made you, you are actually better acquainted with the triune God than you may realize. Don't get too caught up worrying about what you don't know, rejoice in what you do know, and ask God to help you grow in your knowledge of and love for Him.

How are the Father, Son, and Holy Spirit at work in salvation?

Instead of trying to illustrate the Trinity, tell the story of your personal encounter with the Trinity.

2

GOD IS HOLY

ENGAGE

Have you ever been starstruck? It doesn't happen to everyone, but some people have chance encounters with people they really admire, and it leaves them speechless.

Some people on a flight to Los Angeles had an encounter like this with one of their favorite actors: Keanu Reeves. The plane they were in was having a little bit of trouble and needed to make an emergency landing a hundred miles away from their destination. They were going to be trapped at the airport for hours waiting for another flight until Keanu had an idea. He organized a bus trip to get them all home.

The people waiting with him were freaking out a little bit. They were taking videos and posting it to their stories, tweeting about just how crazy it was this was happening to them. They even stopped to take pictures with him as they were waiting for their bus to arrive.[1]

If you could meet someone who would leave you starstruck, who would it be?

SET APART

One of the first things you learn without having to be taught is that you should not stare directly into the sun. It's millions of miles away from us, but it is still too bright to stare into—even while wearing sunglasses.

The great scientist Isaac Newton knew this, but he had the sort of mind that just couldn't take something as fact without trying it himself. One day, he used a mirror to study the sun and its reflection. Spoiler alert: It didn't work. In fact, it almost did permanent damage to his eyes. After staring into the sun, he had to hide in a pitch black room, and still saw the "after-images" when his eyes were closed.[2]

The sun is something completely beyond ordinary people's understanding: It's a white-hot star, much bigger than the earth, hotter than anything we can even imagine, and farther away than humans have ever been (possibly farther than they'll ever go). And we can't even look directly at it without special equipment.

We can still view, measure, and study the sun with special equipment. With some help, we can, get our heads around it. God, on the other hand, is a completely different story. He has a quality that we call "holiness" that we use to describe how set apart from everything else He is. And encountering God's holiness is not something easily forgotten.

Read about Isaiah's response when he saw God in a vision.

> In the year that King Uzziah died, I saw the Lord seated on a high and lofty throne, and the hem of his robe filled the temple. Seraphim were standing above him; they each had six wings: with two they covered their faces, with two they covered their feet, and with two they flew. And one called to another: Holy, holy, holy is the LORD of Armies; his glory fills the whole earth. The foundations of the doorways shook at the sound of their voices, and the temple was filled with smoke. Then I said: Woe is me for I am ruined because I am a man of unclean lips and live among a people of unclean lips, and because my eyes have seen the King, the LORD of Armies.
> **ISAIAH 6:1-5**

What things in this passage show how completely powerful God is?

Why do you think Isaiah reacted this way to seeing God?

INDESCRIBABLE

God's holiness is something we sinful humans simply cannot understand. He is completely perfect, unspeakably powerful, absolutely majestic in ways we can't fully comprehend. Just a mere glimpse of Him broke Isaiah: He called himself ruined!

Not many people throughout history have seen God seated on His throne, but those who did, like Isaiah, struggled to put it into words. Read Revelation 4:2-8 as a group.

John described some pretty crazy things in this passage. Which of them stuck out to you, and why?

Why do you think it is so difficult for people to describe what God looks like?

Everyone who tries to describe God's holiness becomes speechless. Over and over John searched for things to compare to what he was seeing: sometimes animals, sometimes stones, sometimes a sea of glass. When it comes to describing something like God's holiness, sometimes the closest we can get is with metaphors.

One thing that is not difficult to describe about God's holiness is our appropriate response. We should respond to His holiness with reverence and obedience. Obedience is a pretty easy word to understand: Act on what God tells you to do. But reverence has a specific definition that applies especially well here.

Reverence is a profound, awed respect for something. Look back at the response Isaiah had to encountering God's holiness. When looking directly at God's holiness, the only way he knew how to respond was to see himself the way he was: completely, hopelessly lost. There was no way he was ever going to measure up to God's standard on his own. Being in God's presence fundamentally changed him as a person. He went from being an observer of a heavenly scene to feeling completely unworthy of being there in the first place. He had a profound, awed respect for the presence of God.

Have you ever felt God's presence? If you have, how would you describe it?

What did it feel like? How did it change you after you felt it?

HOLINESS DEMANDS OBEDIENCE

After Isaiah experienced deep, profound reverence for the presence of God, something incredible happened.

> *Then one of the seraphim flew to me, and in his hand was a glowing coal that he had taken from the altar with tongs. He touched my mouth with it and said: Now that this has touched your lips, your iniquity is removed and your sin is atoned for. Then I heard the voice of the Lord asking: Who should I send? Who will go for us? I said: Here I am. Send me.*
> **ISAIAH 6:6-8**

After he was cleansed with fire, God asked a question: "Who should I send?"

Isaiah was deeply moved and forever changed by this encounter with the one, true, holy God. He knew he had only one option: to do what God wanted him to do. He didn't even know what it was at the time, but he knew if it was God sending him, he absolutely had to go.

Encountering God is a life-changing experience. Since He reveals Himself to us every day in dozens of different ways, we have opportunity after opportunity to respond to Him with obedience. Once we recognize God is the holy One, He is completely above sinful humanity, and He is fully deserving of our reverence and respect, the only option we have left is to go.

What kinds of things do you think God asks His people to do?

Have you ever felt the need to respond to God in obedience? Tell us about it.

What is something you think God might be leading you to do right now? How can you respond to Him in obedience?

BEING // All people are created in God's image to reflect Him and live in relationship with Him. Sin damaged that image and brought separation, but Christians are new creations with the distinct privilege of enjoying a restored relationship with God and reflecting His character to the world in a special way.

DOING // Because we are created to reflect God and live in relationship with Him, we should continually pursue God in His Word and through prayer, live in continual fellowship within the church, and help people who do not know Him find Him so they can live in fellowship with Him, too.

Living the life of a Christian means living in submission to God's Word, which tells us to "love the Lord your God with all your heart, with all your soul, and with all your mind" (Matt. 28:37) and to "love your neighbor as yourself" (Matt. 28:39). Jesus simplified the entire law down to these two commandments. When we obey these two commands, we find that obeying the rest of God's commands comes naturally. Unfortunately, that's more difficult than it looks. That's why we should wake up every day and take new steps to become more Christlike than we were the day before.

APOLOGETIC // Many today believe there are many gods and many ways to heaven, and that we are free to define God according to our personal perspectives. However, Scripture teaches there is one God (Deut. 6:4).

CHRIST

Jesus is the only holy person who ever lived. In fact, one time He had an encounter with a group of demons who were living inside of and tormenting a man, and even they knew it. They said, "What do you have to do with us, Jesus of Nazareth? Have you come to destroy us? I know who you are—the Holy One of God" (Mark 1:24). Even the demons showed reverence and acknowledged just how Holy Jesus was.

How are you expressing your reverence to Jesus, the Holy One of God, in your everyday life?

COMMUNITY

Just before Jesus left His disciples for the last time before His crucifixion, He gave them one last command: "'As the Father has loved me, I have also loved you. Remain in my love. If you keep my commands you will remain in my love, just as I have kept my Father's commands and remain in his love'" (John 15:9-10). This would inform the way they saw each other and the way they grew His church in the coming years, because starting from the place of love has measurable effects on the people around you. If we want to be obedient to God, we have to have love for the people around us.

Who is someone in your immediate circle—your family or your close friends—who needs to feel the love of Jesus coming from you this week?

Why did you think of this person?

CULTURE

We live in a time that tells us the ultimate goal of our lives is to make ourselves happy. We're told that we are to be our first priority. Scripture tells us the exact opposite: Our first allegiance is to our Creator. We owe Him the firstfruits of our attention and the entirety of our obedience. We worship and obey God because we do not worship and obey ourselves.

How do you see our culture encouraging selfishness?

How does submission to God contradict this?

Session 2

DEVOTIONS

NAME ABOVE ALL NAMES

Jesus is the precise articulation of God's nature. He is rightly given a name above every other name. In terms of hierarchy, Jesus outranks the angels. Consider what the opening chapter of the Book of Hebrews teaches us about Jesus.

> *Long ago God spoke to the fathers by the prophets at different times and in different ways. In these last days, he has spoken to us by his Son. God has appointed him heir of all things and made the universe through him. The Son is the radiance of God's glory and the exact expression of his nature, sustaining all things by his powerful word. After making purification for sins, he sat down at the right hand of the Majesty on high. So he became superior to the angels, just as the name he inherited is more excellent than theirs.*
> **HEBREWS 1:1-4**

In what way did God speak to previous generations before Jesus?

How does He speak to us today?

Take an inventory of your priorities. Does Jesus outrank social media, entertainment, and your appearance in the eyes of your peers? How can you be sure?

Close your eyes and replay your day yesterday. As you consider how you prioritize your time, what has stepped into Jesus' place at the top of your heart's hierarchy?

THE WORD

Knowing about God is not nearly enough. Demons know about God. Stop merely knowing about God. Instead, *know* God. Know Him not in passing, but in the fullness of His Word and in the presence of His Spirit. This is no small thing. To know God in the fullness of how He reveals Himself through His Word is to know the Truth who overcomes the darkness.

> *In the beginning was the Word, and the Word was with God, and the Word was God. He was with God in the beginning. All things were created through him, and apart from him not one thing was created that has been created. In him was life, and that life was the light of men. That light shines in the darkness, and yet the darkness did not overcome it.*
> **JOHN 1:1-5**

Here, John wrote knowing his original Greek audience. Influenced by the conquest of Alexander the Great who propagated Greek thought, the culture of the original readers of John's Gospel were looking for the *Logos*; that rock-solid foundation upon which you could build morality. The word *Logos* in Greek is translated "Word" in English.

We capitalize proper nouns such as the names of people. Why is the word "Word" capitalized in John 1:1?

Why would John use this word when addressing Greek readers?

How did Jesus physically embody the *Logos*, the foundation of truth itself which Greeks sought?

Look back to verse 5. Did the darkness overcome Jesus? Do you think your own personal darkness will be too much for Jesus today? Explain.

THE HOLY SPIRIT

God the Father is the Creator who walked in the Garden of Eden with Adam and Eve. God the Son is Jesus Christ who walked the earth 2,000 years ago. God the Holy Spirit moves our hearts on earth today.

We have seen how Jesus is the Son of God who embodies the Word we read. We have seen God the Father who created all that exists both physically and spiritually. Have you experienced God the Holy Spirit, though? God the Holy Spirit poured out on the New Testament church profoundly in the second chapter of the Book of Acts and then again in the tenth chapter. However, He has existed since the very beginning.

Look at the opening chapter of the Bible.

> Now the earth was formless and empty, darkness covered the surface of the watery depths, and the Spirit of God was hovering over the surface of the waters. Then God said, "Let there be light," and there was light. God saw that the light was good, and God separated the light from the darkness. God called the light "day," and the darkness he called "night." There was an evening, and there was a morning: one day.
>
> **GENESIS 1:2-5**

How would you describe the Holy Spirit in your own words?

Does the idea of being fully known by God scare you or bless you?

When you think about knowing God through His Spirit, what comes to mind?

ENGAGE

LEVELS OF BIBLICAL LEARNING STATEMENT
God is worthy of our worship, and to misplace attention or affections to worldly things which are rightly owed to God is idolatry.

In ancient India, there was an old folktale that went something like this: There were four brothers who each decided to become experts at one specific ability. They spent years on their own perfecting their individual abilities and then came back to tell the others what they'd learned.

The first said, "I have learned how to take the bone out of a creature and create the flesh that goes with it." The second said, "I have learned how to grow skin and hair if there is flesh on its bones." The third said, "If you give me flesh, skin, and hair, I can make limbs." The fourth said, "I have figured out how to make something dead come to life."

They wanted to prove to each other that they'd truly learned these things. They went into the jungle and found the bone of a lion. The first took a bone out of it and added flesh. The second gave it skin and hair. The third gave it matching limbs, and the fourth made it come to life. Unfortunately, none of them knew quite what to do with a live lion, so when it came to life, it roared, ate them, and bounded off into the jungle.[1]

The moral of this story is that if we're not careful, the things we're consumed with can consume us. This is what happens when the things we thirst after and chase with our whole hearts are not the Lord. It's a picture of what, exactly, idolatry is: a pursuit of things that will leave us empty.

What are some examples of things we think will fulfill us but ultimately leave us feeling empty?

WHAT IS WORSHIP?

If you've been in church for any amount of time at all, you've probably heard some version of this: "Stand to your feet and let's worship together." After this, the music starts playing and a song begins.

This is the image many people have of worship. While singing is definitely something you can use to worship, it's not all worship is. Worship is something you do with your entire life— not just the hour or so at a time you spend in a church building.

Let's start with a simple definition straight from the dictionary: "to honor or show reverence for as a divine being or supernatural power."[2] This is just one of the definitions Merriam-Webster came up with. But keep those two things—honor and reverence—in mind as you read these passages aloud:

> For the LORD is great and highly praised; he is feared above all gods. For all the gods of the peoples are idols, but the LORD made the heavens.
> **1 CHRONICLES 16:25-26**

> Give thanks to the LORD, for he is good; his faithful love endures forever.
> **1 CHRONICLES 16:34**

> LORD, you are my God; I will exalt you. I will praise your name, for you have accomplished wonders, plans formed long ago, with perfect faithfulness.
> **ISAIAH 25:1**

> This is why you are great, Lord GOD. There is no one like you, and there is no God besides you, as all we have heard confirms.
> **2 SAMUEL 7:22**

What are some of the reasons these writers say God is worthy to be worshiped?

Why do you think God is worthy to be worshiped?

WORSHIP AND THE GOSPEL

For thousands of years before Jesus came, God had very specific instructions for how His people were to worship Him: through sacrifices. But Jesus offered Himself as a sacrifice on our behalf. We no longer have to sacrifice animals to encounter and be in community with God. But that doesn't mean God changed the way He deserves to be worshiped. He is still deserving of our honor and reverence—only now, the sacrifices are our bodies.

> *Therefore, brothers and sisters, in view of the mercies of God, I urge you to present your bodies as a living sacrifice, holy and pleasing to God; this is your true worship. Do not be conformed to this age, but be transformed by the renewing of your mind, so that you may discern what is the good, pleasing, and perfect will of God.*
> **ROMANS 12:1-2**

Paul said true worship is a pretty simple thing: We offer our bodies as living sacrifices to God because of how in awe we are of who He is. It's not something we do once or twice a week; it's the way we live on a daily basis.

What comes to mind when you hear the word *sacrifice*?

When has someone sacrificed something for you? How did that affect you?

Offering ourselves as sacrifices means we submit to God's will. We aren't supposed to be "conformed to this age," but are, instead, supposed to be "transformed" by renewing our minds. God is holy: He is set apart and completely above us. Notice what Paul said: as we live as sacrifices we are also to be "holy." There's that word again: *holy*. But this time, it's talking about something we are supposed to be.

Of course, there is no way we could ever be holy the way God is. But that's the type of sacrifice God deserves. He deserves us to be wholly, completely devoted to Him. Unfortunately, we miss the mark of holiness all the time.

What do you think it means to live a life "holy and pleasing to God"? Why is it so difficult to live this way?

THE DANGER OF IDOLATRY

The problem of falling short of holy living has been around for a long time. In fact, one of the best examples of what it looks like to miss this mark comes from the Book of Jeremiah.

> *For my people have committed a double evil: They have abandoned me, the fountain of living water, and dug cisterns for themselves—cracked cisterns that cannot hold water.*
> **JEREMIAH 2:13**

Before saying this, God talked about how sad it was that Israel turned its affection away from Him. They stopped seeking His face. They stopped asking for His wisdom. He says they exchanged the glory of God for "useless idols" (Jer. 2:11). Then He explained their situation using a metaphor they could understand: water from a well.

We can get behind this image even if we haven't seen a cistern or a well before. If God is the clean, living water, then the people have abandoned it for a dirty, makeshift, cracked well that can't even hold water. Instead of worshiping the God who made them, who sustains them, and who is worthy of worship, they have turned to other things that stand no chance of satisfying them.

Sin is basically idolatry, or putting something in the place only God should hold. For some, it is fame and recognition. For others, it is wealth and success. It might be as simple as the affection of someone they wish were interested in them or gratifying desires they know go against God's Word. All sin is idolatry because it tells God, "my wants, my desires, and my rules are more important than yours."

How do you see people putting other things in the place only God should have in their lives?

What are you tempted to focus on instead of God?

What is one way you can offer yourself as a living sacrifice to God this week?

God never changes. He never stops being worthy of our total affection and all of our devotion. We are imperfect and each one of us constantly falls short of His standard, but if we wake up every day asking God to teach us to give ourselves entirely to Him, we can grow steadily into the kind of people who worship Him the way He deserves to be worshiped.

BEING // All people are created in God's image to reflect Him and live in relationship with Him. Sin damaged that image and brought separation, but Christians are new creations with the distinct privilege of enjoying a restored relationship with God and reflecting His character to the world in a special way. Every time you wake up is a new opportunity to realign the affections of your heart so that they are in tune with the One who made you. Too often we find ourselves running to the "cracked cisterns" of popularity or self-indulgence because they promise to make us feel whole. But they never do. You will never feel more full, more quenched, than when you place God on the throne of your life and let Him direct your steps.

DOING // Because we are created to reflect God and live in relationship with Him, we should continually pursue God in His Word and through prayer, live in continual fellowship within the church, and help people who do not know Him find Him so they can live in fellowship with Him, too.

APOLOGETIC // Many today believe there are many gods and many ways to heaven, and that we are free to define God according to our personal perspectives. However, Scripture teaches there is one God (Deut. 6:4).

CHRIST

Jesus told a woman if she drank from the water He gave her, it would "become a well of water springing up in him for eternal life" (John 4:14). He didn't mean she wouldn't have to drink physical water; He was talking about the kind of water her soul needed. Every person's soul is thirsty for something, and so many of us run to all kinds of places trying to quench it. The problem is that all of those roads eventually lead to ruin. When we find our identity, our delight, and our purpose in Christ, we'll find ourselves being fulfilled in a way only He can.

When are you prone to wander from the Lord and look for satisfaction elsewhere?

What steps can you take to turn from that and focus on Him?

COMMUNITY

One of the perks of surrounding ourselves with like-minded brothers and sisters is that we can hold each other up as we become more like Christ. That's one of the things gospel-centered community is best at. The author of Hebrews told the church to do the following: "watch out for one another to provoke love and good works, not neglecting to gather together, as some are in the habit of doing, but encouraging each other" (Heb. 10:24-25).

What does it look like to "provoke love and good works" in each other?

Do you have a community like this in your life now? What can you do to make it happen?

CULTURE

Some have referred to the church as something like a hospital for sick people. A place people can come when they have nowhere else to turn, when they've reached the ends of their ropes. While we absolutely want to be a place where people are welcome no matter what they look like and no matter what situation they're in, that isn't what God put us here for. Paul said God "gave some to be apostles, some prophets, some evangelists, some pastors and teachers, equipping the saints for the work of ministry, to build up the body of Christ" (Eph. 4:11-12).

The body of Christ isn't a hospital; it's an incubator—a controlled environment used for the growth of new organisms or special care of weak organisms. Simply put: The church is a place designed to help followers of Jesus grow. It's where people can encounter God and be equipped to be gospel outposts in the middle of people who don't believe. Let's build each other up so we can be sent out as shining examples of what happens when God gets one hundred percent of our lives.

What do you think the purpose of the church is?

How can we use a community of believers to reach the unbelieving culture around us?

Session 3

DEVOTIONS

THE COMING OF THE HOLY SPIRIT

At the Tower of Babel, to protect mankind from our own accelerating our sinfulness, God confused our speech, causing people to speak different languages. Then, at the dawn of the New Covenant era, God did something remarkable. He temporarily lifted the language barrier so the gospel would make its way into every culture of the earth.

When the day of Pentecost had arrived, they were all together in one place. Suddenly a sound like that of a violent rushing wind came from heaven, and it filled the whole house where they were staying. They saw tongues like flames of fire that separated and rested on each one of them. Then they were all filled with the Holy Spirit and began to speak in different tongues, as the Spirit enabled them. Now there were Jews staying in Jerusalem, devout people from every nation under heaven. When this sound occurred, a crowd came together and was confused because each one heard them speaking in his own language.
ACTS 2:1-6

Jesus told His disciples it would be better for them if He ascended to heaven for precisely this reason. He knew the Holy Spirit was going to come down as He ascended to heaven. He called the Holy Spirit "Counselor," giving us another name for God and a deeper look into how He would help us understand and remember things about Him (John 14:26).

Describe the Holy Spirit, according to this passage.

Journal a story of your walk with the Spirit so far.

What do you believe the Holy Spirit of God may do through you in the future?

IN SPIRIT AND IN TRUTH

God is Spirit and so the act of worshiping God is a spiritual act. Listen in on this pivotal conversation between Jesus and the Samaritan woman at the well. The woman thought Jesus was going to weigh in on a centuries-old debate between Jews and their Samaritan relatives. Was the ancient altar set by Abraham still the place to worship or was Jerusalem really the location to carry out Old Testament sacrifices.

Jesus took neither stance, but instead ushered in an entirely new view of worship for our New Testament era.

> *Jesus told her, "Believe me, woman, an hour is coming when you will worship the Father neither on this mountain nor in Jerusalem. You Samaritans worship what you do not know. We worship what we do know, because salvation is from the Jews. But an hour is coming, and is now here, when the true worshipers will worship the Father in Spirit and in truth. Yes, the Father wants such people to worship him. God is spirit, and those who worship him must worship in Spirit and in truth."*
> **JOHN 4:21-24**

What does it mean to worship God in Spirit?

What does it mean to worship God in truth?

BE HOLY

Some of the attributes of God that are relevant to us and that we can wrap our heads around in a meaningful capacity are His holiness, His goodness, His kindness, His omnipotence, and His sovereignty. These attributes will take some time to unpack.

Things exist that are above, separated, and anointed as more cherished than anything else in this life. We call these things "holy." God's holiness is perfect. He has absolute integrity. He positively never ever slips up.

There in His holiness, He invites us to join Him. This is a huge deal because we have all been born with a sinful nature. We are the beloved, messy sinners whose Savior is perfect. This may be overwhelming to consider, but it is important to face it head-on.

> *For it is written, Be holy, because I am holy.*
> **1 PETER 1:16**

There it is. God is holy and calls us to be holy as well. Now, do not be discouraged. By the power of the Holy Spirit, God can make us more like Him. It is daunting and a wrong thought pattern to try to alter your behavior as you aspire to perfection, so be sure you do not misinterpret this call to holiness. Holiness is the standard. We are well below it. So, we need a Savior.

In your own words, describe God's holiness.

List ways you have seen the Holy Spirit bring about holiness in your life.

GOD THE CREATOR

ENGAGE

One of the most famous composers of all time is Johann Sebastian Bach. Odds are, you've heard music he composed. If you've ever seen someone playing an organ in a movie, there's a good chance they're playing "Toccata and Fugue in D Minor." If you looked online for it right now and found a video of someone playing it, you would likely immediately recognize it. He's inspired countless composers, musicians, and artists for hundreds of years and is considered by many to be one of the greatest composers of all time.

But whenever he finished writing a piece of music, just before he signed his name at the bottom, he would include three letters: SDG. This stands for the Latin phrase *Soli Deo Gloria,* which means "to God alone be the glory." Bach knew that when people heard his music, they were hearing something bigger than just the notes. They were listening to greatness, and he wanted to make sure that the greatness they recognized was not his, but God's.[1]

If you could be known for anything, what would you want it to be?

Bach was a brilliant creator of music, but he doesn't hold a candle to God—the supreme Creator of all. And just like Bach's music pointed people to God, so does God's creation. Since we are God's crowning achievement, we have a responsibility to reflect the glory of the One who created us and the privilege of enjoying a relationship with Him.

IN THE BEGINNING

Creators have been signing their work for as long as they've been making it.
But did you know we are signed by our Creator, too? That's one of the most spectacular things about God. Not only did He make everything, He made sure it all pointed back to Him. Let's see how He did this.

In the beginning God created the heavens and the earth.
GENESIS 1:1

The whole first chapter of Genesis tells an amazing story: the story of how we came to be. The story of how *everything* came to be. It was written down so a group of people surrounded by foreign nations with all kinds of ideas about how the Universe came into existence could know who was truly responsible for it all: God.

Look at some of the creation myths that were going around at the time when this was written:
- The Babylonians believed that there was a great battle between different gods and that one of the gods, Tiamat, was killed and split in half with an arrow. Marduk—the god who defeated her, is said to have created the heavens and earth with her body.[2]
- One Egyptian myth said that there were two creatures, a Chaos Goose and Chaos Gander (a male goose) that came together and created an egg—and that egg was the Sun. The gander was also identified with the earth god, Seb.[3]
- In Norse mythology, it is said that the three Gods—Odin, Vili, and Ve—killed a frost giant. They cut his body into pieces, and different parts of the Universe were born of each piece. But this isn't just a Norse tradition, many cultures believe in this kind of earth beginning.[4]

What are other ideas you've heard about the way the Universe came to be?

How does the Bible's creation account clear up any confusion about how the Universe was made?

MADE IN GOD'S IMAGE

The beginning of the most important book on the planet begins by cutting straight to the chase. It says, in essence, "Hey, I know you're hearing lots of things from a lot of people around you about random happenstance, wars between gods, and all kinds of stuff, but don't get this wrong: God made everything. He was here in the beginning, and all of creation is a result of His work."

But the Bible's account of creation tells us something even more incredible than just who made the Universe. It tells who made us. It even records God's intentions when He did it. Take a look at what God did when He made people.

> Then God said, "Let us make man in our image, according to our likeness. They will rule the fish of the sea, the birds of the sky, the livestock, the whole earth, and the creatures that crawl on the earth." So God created man in his own image; he created him in the image of God; he created them male and female. God blessed them, and God said to them, "Be fruitful, multiply, fill the earth, and subdue it. Rule the fish of the sea, the birds of the sky, and every creature that crawls on the earth."
> **GENESIS 1:26-28**

God gave people something He hadn't given anything else in all of the Universe. He gave them His image.

This word "image" is interesting. It comes from a word pretty similar to "icon," something you are probably very familiar with. On your phone, if you want to open an app, you have to touch an icon: an image that points you in the direction of the app you want to open. In the same way, people are the image of God because we point to the One who created us.

This doesn't mean we physically look like God. He doesn't have a body like ours or anything like that. Instead, it means we have things God has, which nothing else in creation has. We can make rational decisions, we can think about things like good and evil, we can examine our place in our communities, in nature, and in the Universe. We are His image-bearers on the Earth.

Why is it so easy to think of ourselves as not special, ordinary, or "less than" someone else?

How does knowing you are God's image-bearer affect the way you see yourself?

HIS CROWNING ACHIEVEMENT

Being God's image-bearers means something deeper than what we have; it also tells us something about what we are. God put people on Earth as His crowning achievement, as His representatives among the things He created. Then, He gave them a direct command: "Be fruitful, multiply, fill the earth, and subdue it" (Gen. 1:28). God wanted to fill the planet He made with the representatives of His image. He wanted us to reflect His glory everywhere!

Later in the Bible, God said:

I will say to the north, 'Give them up!' and to the south, 'Do not hold them back!' Bring my sons from far away, and my daughters from the ends of the earth—everyone who bears my name and is created for my glory. I have formed them; indeed, I have made them."
ISAIAH 43:6-7

Is it comforting to you to know God specifically designed you to bear His image? Why or why not?

But He didn't just make us to reflect His glory; He created us to have a relationship with Him. Revelation 4:11 says, "Our Lord and God, you are worthy to receive glory and honor and power, because you have created all things, and by your will they exist and were created." We were created by His will. He didn't have to create us, but He wanted to, so He did.

I will walk among you and be your God, and you will be my people.
LEVITICUS 26:12

"See what great love the Father has given us that we should be called God's children—and we are!"
1 JOHN 3:1a

You are special because God, the Creator of all things, made *you*. You are part of His crowning achievement, and you have been given the honor of enjoying a relationship with Him. There can be no greater calling in the world.

BEING // All people are created in God's image to reflect Him and live in relationship with Him. Sin damaged that image and brought separation, but Christians are new creations with the distinct privilege of enjoying a restored relationship with God and reflecting His character to the world in a special way.

DOING // Because we are created to reflect God and live in relationship with Him, we should continually pursue God in His Word and through prayer, live in continual fellowship within the church, and help people who do not know Him find Him so they can live in fellowship with Him, too.

APOLOGETIC // Many today believe there are many gods and many ways to heaven, and that we are free to define God according to our personal perspectives. However, Scripture teaches there is one God (Deut. 6:4).

   The very first verse in the whole Bible was no less controversial at the time it was written than it is today. The ultimate question we can answer is who created us. If we were a chaotic accident in a Universe without rules—nothing but pure happenstance— then we owe our allegiance to nothing but ourselves. If we were created, then that changes everything.

   The logic follows like this: Nothing exists without someone (or something) making it. We have a physical world around us. Since the world exists, someone (or something) had to have made it. Scripture makes it clear from the very beginning who made it. Creation implies a Creator. We have one, and He wants a relationship with us.

CHRIST

Paul wrote to the church at Corinth, "for us there is one God, the Father. All things are from him, and we exist for him. And there is one Lord, Jesus Christ. All things are through him, and we exist through him" (1 Cor. 8:6). Think about how incredible it is that we can know our Savior, who is also the very reason we exist in the first place! But cultivating a relationship with Him is not something that happens by accident. It's a daily task, one you have to devote yourself to each moment of the day. By ourselves, we want to bring ourselves glory, but as we cast our eyes to Jesus and become more like Him, we reflect His glory instead.

What are things you struggle with when it comes to walking with the Lord daily?

COMMUNITY

God created mankind in His image—that doesn't mean just you, it means the people sitting next to you. It means the people who live across the street, the people you see in movies, the people you'll never meet in your life. We were made to have a relationship with our Creator, but we were also made to have a relationship with one another. We can embrace our differences because we share the most important thing in common: We have the same Father. This common ground should be the backbone to every one of our interactions and the lens through which we see the many ways we're different.

What's a baby step you can take to either begin a relationship with Him, get back on track after being away for a while, or take bigger steps toward Him than you did yesterday?

How can we help each other prioritize our relationship with the Lord?

CULTURE

It's hard to imagine looking at a world more divided than ours is. As a culture, we find any reason at all to be more distant from each other. We argue about everything from politics to sports team affiliations, widening the divide between us at every turn. Christ does the exact opposite of that. When we see that we are all children of God who have one Creator and one Lord, and that all of humanity has one purpose—to enjoy a relationship with Him—those little things tend to fall to the side. That doesn't mean we'll always agree everything, but even our disagreements will be filtered through the lens that we are all in the exact same boat. We are all creations of the same Creator, and Jesus died for the person next to you just as much as He died for you.

Do you agree that the world is growing more divided? Why or why not?

How does the gospel provide a remedy for this division?

Session 4

DEVOTIONS

TASTE AND SEE

Taste and see that the LORD is good. How happy is the person who takes refuge in him!
PSALM 34:8

The first sentence of this verse is an invitation. Did you notice that? You have been invited into fellowship with God. When Jesus' birth was prophesied, it was said that He would be "Immanuel" which means "God is with us" (Matt. 1:23). He is not a distant Creator: He is the intimate Savior. He is near and He is good.

The goodness of God is such a vital attribute as far as we are concerned. How different the Universe would be if God were all-powerful and sovereign, but not good. We are blessed to know our God is absolutely good.

He is good even when our circumstances are not. It is so important that you write this upon your heart (Prov. 3:3). God is absolutely good. God is always good. Trust in the goodness of God and let it illuminate the eternal finish line on the horizon.

Taste and see that the Lord is good by fellowshipping with Him, reading His Word, and abiding in His Spirit. Your life on earth may be gritty, but knowing your God is good will help you endure it.

Describe a season of your life in which you questioned the goodness of God. What was happening in your life at that time?

Is God under any obligation to make your life easier? Would you think more highly of His goodness if your life were better?

ETERNALLY POWERFUL

Dirt does not create itself. Matter does not generate itself. It is obviously impossible that our universe would create itself, yet here we are. Out of nothingness comes absolutely nothing, yet the Universe exists. To test this, all you need is an empty box. Stare at an empty box for one hour or nine trillion hours. In either case, nothing will spring into existence out of that box.

We all know this, but people live as though the Universe created itself. Why? It is not because that is logical at all. Rather, it is because we just want to get away with sin. Here is how Paul described the issue:

> *For God's wrath is revealed from heaven against all godlessness and unrighteousness of people who by their unrighteousness suppress the truth, since what can be known about God is evident among them, because God has shown it to them. For his invisible attributes, that is, his eternal power and divine nature, have been clearly seen since the creation of the world, being understood through what he has made. As a result, people are without excuse.*
> **ROMANS 1:18-20**

God is eternally powerful. He exists outside of time itself. He must; otherwise, the universe could not physically exist. God is timeless and uncreated. If you were to graph out His life, it would not be an endless line, but a fixed point in space. He has no beginning and no end.

What does God's timeless nature indicate about His perspective on your problems? Is He overwhelmed by them?

Why do you think some people believe the Universe created itself and that life generated itself, despite evidence of a Creator?

GOD IS IN CHARGE

God is in charge. None of the other attributes of God would matter if God were not sovereign. It would be meaningless for us if God were kind, holy, and all-powerful, but disconnected from us. We are so blessed to worship the one true God who is holy, good, and in-control.

In the Book of Revelation, John gives a vivid prophetic picture of Jesus as He truly is. Look to the immense title He is given in this passage. Not only is He King, He is the King over all other kings. Not only is He Lord, He is Lord over all other lords of this world:

> Then I saw heaven opened, and there was a white horse. Its rider is called *Faithful and True, and he judges and makes war with justice. His eyes were like a fiery flame, and many crowns were on his head. He had a name written that no one knows except himself. He wore a robe dipped in blood, and his name is called the Word of God. The armies that were in heaven followed him on white horses, wearing pure white linen. A sharp sword came from his mouth, so that he might strike the nations with it. He will rule them with an iron rod. He will also trample the winepress of the fierce anger of God, the Almighty. And he has a name written on his robe and on his thigh: KING OF KINGS AND LORD OF LORDS.*
> **REVELATION 19:11-16**

List the things of this world that are overwhelming for you.

Now, compare that list with this description of Jesus. Can you endure a little longer knowing your God is sovereign and will return to conquer all that is evil?

SPIRITUAL DISCIPLINES : 5

ENGAGE

The Five Love Languages by Gary Chapman asserts that everybody has at least one way they prefer to be told that they're loved. There are five basic categories:

- **Words of Affirmation:** You like it best when people tell you things with their words that build you up.
- **Physical Touch:** You're the type that would take a hug over a handshake any time.
- **Quality Time:** What matters to you isn't so much what you do with someone, you just like being with them.
- **Gifts:** You feel most cared for when people are giving you gifts that remind you they thought of you.
- **Acts of Service:** If someone wants to tell you they care, they'll do something for you.[1]

Which of these makes you feel most loved?

Which of these describes how you'd prefer to tell someone that they're loved?

We are built for communication because we were made by a God who communicates with us all the time. Communicating with the people around us takes some practice, and it can be the same when we're learning how to communicate with God.

THE INSPIRED WORD

God communicates with us through many ways than this. He directs circumstances, speaks to us through other people, and tells us about Himself through the world around us. But He communicates with us even more directly through His Word, which He has already given us.

What is something you've struggled with when it comes to the Bible?

Who can help you when you have struggles with the Bible?

When Paul wrote his second letter to Timothy, he said, "all Scripture is inspired by God and is profitable for teaching, for rebuking, for correcting, for training in righteousness, so that the man of God may be complete, equipped for every good work" (2 Tim. 3:16-17). For thousands of years, God interacted with people through prophets and leaders who recorded His words and preserved them for us today.

See, God speaks to us most clearly through His Word. He's always spoken to us through His Word. The prophets wrote recorded His Word. The Word of the Lord came to Moses in a burning bush (Ex. 3), and it came to Jonah on the beach after being swallowed by a fish (Jon. 2:10–3:1). The Word guided David as he led Israel (Ps. 19:7), and it puts those who think themselves wise to shame (Jer. 8:9).

God's Word came in its most incredible form about 2,000 years ago:

> *The Word became flesh and dwelt among us. We observed his glory, the glory as the one and only Son from the Father, full of grace and truth.*
> **JOHN 1:14**

In that passage, John called Jesus the *living* Word of God *who* became flesh! Fortunately for us, people penned the things He said and did while He was with them on earth.

What are some things you know about what Jesus did?

Do you have a favorite passage in Scripture about Him? If so, what is it?

GOD SPEAKS

To the Roman church, Paul wrote "Faith comes from what is heard, and what is heard comes through the message about Christ" (Rom. 10:17). Think about this for a second: Our faith comes from hearing the message of Christ—the very same message recorded for us many times over in Scripture! God's Word is the primary method He uses to communicate with us. When we read it, we are hearing words directly from His mouth.

Look at what the writer of Hebrews says:

> For the word of God is living and effective and sharper than any double-edged sword, penetrating as far as the separation of soul and spirit, joints and marrow. It is able to judge the thoughts and intentions of the heart.
> **HEBREWS 4:12**

How incredible is it that Scripture is not just a collection of dead letters, but is alive, able to reach across centuries and cultures and barriers to meet us where we are today? There is no other book on the planet like the Bible, able to be used by so many people for such a long period of time to help people grow into the image of God, because it's the only book breathed by God, Himself. If you want to get to know God, you need to start by getting into His Word.

But communication with God is not a one-way street with us just taking in His Words. God speaks to us in Scripture and invites us to speak to Him in prayer.

Jesus was the absolute best example of what it looks like to have a healthy prayer life. Nobody did it quite like He did. Look up these passages and see if you can identify what He prayed for in each of them:

- **John 17:20-23:**   - **Luke 22:39-46:**   - **Matthew 6:9-13:**

- **Luke 22:31-32:**   - **Matthew 5:44:**   - **Luke 11:2-4:**

In fact, before any major event in Jesus' life, He was always found praying.

What are your thoughts or experiences regarding prayer?

Why do you think that prayer is important? What kinds of things should we pray for?

PRAYER: COMMUNICATING WITH GOD

Prayer was such an important part of Jesus' life that His disciples couldn't help but ask Him about it. They asked Him for advice about how to pray, and He gave it to them. This is the way Jesus taught His disciples how to pray:

> He said to them, "Whenever you pray, say, Father, your name be honored as holy. Your kingdom come. Give us each day our daily bread. And forgive us our sins, for we ourselves also forgive everyone in debt to us. And do not bring us into temptation."
> **LUKE 11:2-4**

He didn't mean for us to always pray these exact words but to always pray for these things.

- **Acknowledge God as King.** He is holy. He is set apart. If you don't know where to start when praying, this is always good place to begin.
- **Depend on God.** This does not mean we depend on God to give us riches or miraculously drop the answers to an upcoming test in our laps; it means we ask Him to provide us with the nourishment we need to grow—both physically and spiritually.
- **Ask for forgiveness.** Every one of us has sinned before God, but we don't have to offer a burnt sacrifice or go before a priest in confession to ask for His forgiveness; you can do it right there in your seat. Right now.
- **Behave excellently toward each other.** If you want to treat others better, start by praying about it. You'll be surprised what God does when you do.

Communication with God—both hearing from Him and speaking to Him—are known as spiritual disciplines. You get better at them the more you practice. And the more you practice, the more of God you will experience. The more of God you experience, the better you'll know Him, and the more you'll want to know Him.

As a believer, spiritual maturity is the ultimate goal—so much so that Paul couldn't stop praying for it (Col. 1:9-10). We should keep praying for God to do the same work in us.

Why should we want to be more spiritually mature? How can we grow spiritually?

How do you think a spiritually mature person would act toward their family members? Toward their friends? Toward complete strangers?

BEING // All people are created in God's image to reflect Him and live in relationship with Him. Sin damaged that image and brought separation, but Christians are new creations with the distinct privilege of enjoying a restored relationship with God and reflecting His character to the world in a special way.

DOING // Because we are created to reflect God and live in relationship with Him, we should continually pursue God in His Word and through prayer, live in continual fellowship within the church, and help people who do not know Him find Him so they can live in fellowship with Him, too.

When we continually practice Scripture reading and memorization, prayer, worship, service, fasting, and building godly community, we are doing something like spiritual exercise. Things like these are called spiritual disciplines because they require focus and effort. You don't have to be an expert in these things overnight; you can start small. Begin by waking up and spending a few minutes reading God's Word and then praying He would use it to make you more like Him. As you make this a habit, you will see that practicing them not only gets easier, but becomes an essential part of your life.

APOLOGETIC // Many today believe there are many gods and many ways to heaven, and that we are free to define God according to our personal perspectives. However, Scripture teaches there is one God (Deut. 6:4).

CHRIST

Building a relationship with Jesus is like building a relationship with your friend. If you do not see each other, speak to one another, understand what each other is saying, or spend time together, it's not very likely you'll have much of a relationship at all. But if our friendships here on earth are worth the effort it takes to maintain them, how much more important should it be to maintain a relationship with the One who saved us? Fortunately, there are spiritual disciplines we can practice which will make growing that relationship easier.

Here are a few of the spiritual disciplines: Bible study, prayer, fasting, confession of sin, worship, fellowship, service, giving, evangelism. Which of them do you find easiest? Which do you find most difficult? Which is one you can focus on beginning right away?

COMMUNITY

If you look at the people around you, odds are they struggle with many of the same things you struggle with. Nobody ever said following Jesus was supposed to be easy. In fact, He Himself said it would be tough. He said that if we want to follow Him, the first thing we have to do is die to ourselves (Luke 9:23). Fortunately, we're all in the same boat, and that means we can help one another where we're weak. This is the root of Christian community. We are all chasing the same goal, so we shouldn't be shy about admitting the places we struggle. It'd be a safe bet to say you are far from alone in this struggle.

Why is it difficult to admit to people that we're struggling with something?

What benefits do you think would come from admitting our shortcomings to one another?

CULTURE

So much of what we see around us is mundane. If something is mundane, it is temporary, ordinary or ultimately unimportant. Think of just how dreary it would be to spend an entire life waking up, trudging through daily tasks, and finding some desperate way to entertain ourselves before falling asleep again? Though it looks different for almost everyone, a lot of people live this way. Now, think about the life of a believer. We aren't exempt from the ordinary things of life, but we can do such things with a bigger purpose. We were created for something huge: a relationship with the one who created us!

And we get to model something for a world desperately searching for meaning and purpose. We can show them what it's like to live for something much bigger and better than ourselves.

Is it refreshing to have something bigger to live for than just yourself? Why or why not?

How can you model for the people in your everyday life you live for something bigger than yourself?

Session 5

DEVOTIONS

GOD IS ALL POWERFUL

No mountain is too big for God to move. No person is too broken for Him to heal. No circumstance, disease, or disaster is too much for Him to overcome. This is what it means to be omnipotent. He is absolutely all-powerful.

In the Book of Revelation, Jesus took the scroll that is the title deed to fallen creation. He is able to redeem us. Take a look at what happened when He took the scroll.

When he took the scroll, the four living creatures and the twenty-four elders fell down before the Lamb. Each one had a harp and golden bowls filled with incense, which are the prayers of the saints. And they sang a new song: You are worthy to take the scroll and to open its seals, because you were slaughtered, and you purchased people for God by your blood from every tribe and language and people and nation. You made them a kingdom and priests to our God, and they will reign on the earth. Then I looked and heard the voice of many angels around the throne, and also of the living creatures and of the elders. Their number was countless thousands, plus thousands of thousands.
REVELATION 5:8-11

Is there anything too big for God? Try to imagine God's perspective on your problems. Do they overwhelm Him?

What needs to change in your prayer life in light of God's omnipotence?

GOD LOVES YOU

God is the embodiment of love. It is possible and even common to believe in God's power, God's goodness, God's holiness, and God's timelessness while not believing in God's love. This exquisite passage speaks directly to another important attribute of God's.

> *Dear friends, let us love one another, because love is from God, and everyone who loves has been born of God and knows God. The one who does not love does not know God, because God is love. God's love was revealed among us in this way: God sent his one and only Son into the world so that we might live through him. Love consists in this: not that we loved God, but that he loved us and sent his Son to be the atoning sacrifice for our sins. Dear friends, if God loved us in this way, we also must love one another. No one has ever seen God. If we love one another, God remains in us and his love is made complete in us.*
> **1 JOHN 4:7-12**

This is crucial. John's writing is explicitly clear: If you do not have love, you do not know God. Now, do not merely check this box and move on. Press it to your heart. It is one thing to have a theoretical knowledge of God's love. It is quite another to believe on the love of God and show God's love to others when they have brutally wronged you.

Name some people you need to truly love in light of this text.

What needs to shift in your heart? In what ways have you been only nice to people rather than authentically loving them the way a Christian ought to love people?

GOD IS GOOD

God is kind. He could be mean. He has the freedom to be anything imaginable, but He chooses to be kind. In fact, we get our own idea of kindness from God's kindness. If God were not kind, we would likely not have any idea of what kindness is and would be terrible to one another. Instead, we appreciate kindness and emulate God's kindness as we treat one another well.

So, when you see one person being kind to another person, you're seeing a reenactment of the kindness of our Creator God in that person. God created us in His image, so we resemble Him in these ways.

Left to our own devices, defaulting to the sinful nature of our flesh, we will treat one another badly. However, because of the work of the Spirit of God, we see kindness flourish. In writing to the church of Galatia, Paul articulated it this way:

> But the fruit of the Spirit is love, joy, peace, patience, kindness, goodness, faithfulness, gentleness, and self-control. The law is not against such things. Now those who belong to Christ Jesus have crucified the flesh with its passions and desires. If we live by the Spirit, let us also keep in step with the Spirit.
> **GALATIANS 5:22-25**

So, let your heart rest. Breathe out a sigh of gratitude because God is kind. We see kindness exuded from God's people when they are filled with God's Spirit. Did you notice the word "kindness" (v. 22)? When godly people walk in step with the Holy Spirit, they exude and imitate this beautiful attribute of God's and that is kindness.

Apart from God, can you give a reason to be kind? Explain.

As you look at your calendar for the coming week, what are some opportunities to show kindness?

6

THE GREATNESS OF OUR GOD

ENGAGE

LEVELS OF BIBLICAL LEARNING STATEMENT
God is omnipresent (all places at all times), omniscient (all-knowing), and omnipotent (all-powerful), and exercises sovereignty over all creation.

A high school student and his friends had backed their cars into a circle in a mostly empty parking garage. They opened their trunks and sat around strumming guitars, telling stories, and playing their favorite songs over their car speakers. When the student got home later that night, his mother greeted him at the top of the stairs and said, "I heard you were in a parking garage tonight. What were you up to?"

They hadn't been getting into trouble, but it reinforced something he had suspected for a while: his mother was a wizard and could see everything he was up to at any given moment. It must've been a handy skill for her to have as a mother.

Have you ever had an experience like that—where your parents knew what you were up to even if you didn't think it was possible?

Of course, she couldn't see everything he was doing; someone had probably just called and told her what was going on. But at least in the back of his mind, his mother felt omniscient: there was nothing she didn't know. With God this is not the case. But His traits don't stop there. Not only is He omniscient (all-knowing), He is omnipresent (all places at all times) and omnipotent (all-powerful). Let's take a second to look at what these three big words mean.

If you could see like God does just one time—where you can see anything in the past, present, or future anywhere in the Universe—what would you like to see?

OMNIPRESENT

Omnipresent is a word that is actually made up of two words: omni (all) and present. David meditated on this quality of God often, but take a look at what he said in this psalm:

> *Where can I go to escape your Spirit? Where can I flee from your presence? If I go up to heaven, you are there; if I make my bed in Sheol, you are there. If I live at the eastern horizon or settle at the western limits, even there your hand will lead me; your right hand will hold on to me.*
> **PSALM 139:7-10**

He used a lot of poetic imagery in this psalm, but he was driving home the point that there is nowhere we can go to escape God's Spirit. No matter where you are, no matter how far away you think you've run or what kind of situation you've found yourself in you are not far enough away to escape God's presence. Scripture is full of this truth. (Check out 1 Kings 8:27, Proverbs 15:3, and Jeremiah 23:24, just to name a few.)

You might notice God's omnipresence seems like a warning sometimes. But God's it is not meant to be a threat—it is simply the truth about who He is. And the good news is it's an extremely encouraging thing for us. Take a look:

> *"Go, therefore, and make disciples of all nations, baptizing them in the name of the Father and of the Son and of the Holy Spirit, teaching them to observe everything I have commanded you. And remember, I am with you always, to the end of the age."*
> **MATTHEW 28:19-20**

No matter what God calls you to do, He will always be there to strengthen you as you do it. No matter how far you run, you'll never be too far away to escape Him, and He'll never be too far away to hear you.

How does knowing that God is everywhere affect the way you live?

Why is it encouraging that you can't go somewhere God is not?

OMNISCIENT

One of the best parts about getting older is knowing more. But the problem with learning new things is that the more you know, the more you realize how much you don't know. Sometimes learning something new just brings up more questions than answers.

Not so with God. Saying God is omniscient means He is all (*omni*)-knowing (*scient*). There's nothing He doesn't know. There's no secret too deep, no thought too obscure, no mystery unsolved. He knows everything about the past, the present, and the future. Look at a couple of places Scripture explains this to us:

> *He counts the number of the stars; he gives names to all of them. Our Lord is great, vast in power; his understanding is infinite.*
> **PSALM 147:4-5**

> *This is how we will know that we belong to the truth and will reassure our hearts before him whenever our hearts condemn us; for God is greater than our hearts, and he knows all things.*
> **1 JOHN 3:19-20**

> *Before a word is on my tongue, you know all about it, LORD.*
> **PSALM 139:4**

> *"Lord, you know everything; you know that I love you."*
> **JOHN 21:17**

God's omniscience reaches from the stars to the number of hairs on your head. There isn't a corner of creation He has not already understood—because He made it. There is not a step you can take that He doesn't know about—because He has seen it. God knows infinitely more than we will ever be able to comprehend. There are billions of people on this planet; even more grains of sand on the beach, and even more stars in the sky—and He knows all of them.

If you could tap into God's knowledge, what would you like to know?

How does it comfort you to know there's nothing God doesn't know?

OMNIPOTENT

God's all-ness doesn't stop with being everywhere and knowing everything. The third part of His nature is that there's nothing He can't do: He is all powerful, or omnipotent. Just look around you. Look up at the night sky. Look at the way your body works. Feel the tremble of an earthquake, the awe of a hurricane, the power of an erupting volcano. If God is able to make all of that out of nothing, then what in the world could He not do?

Read what Job had to say about God's power.

God is wise and all-powerful. Who has opposed him and come out unharmed? He removes mountains without their knowledge, overturning them in his anger. He shakes the earth from its place so that its pillars tremble. He commands the sun not to shine and seals off the stars. He alone stretches out the heavens and treads on the waves of the sea. He makes the stars: the Bear, Orion, the Pleiades, and the constellations of the southern sky. He does great and unsearchable things, wonders without number.
JOB 9:4-10

Understanding God's omnipotence should cause us to do at least two things:

- **Worship Him.** You serve the highest Power in all creation. Any sense of majesty you get from anything you've ever seen is nothing but a speck in the portrait of how awe-inspiring God is. Consider how majestic He is, and let it fill you with wonder at the God you serve.

- **Fear Him.** This does not mean be afraid of Him; rather, it means treat Him with the respect He deserves, the same way we respect the power of a storm or an avalanche. God is not a genie in a bottle; He is the creator of the Universe, and He is faithful and just to rule the Universe His way.

How does knowing more about God inspire us to worship Him?

How can we worship—and fear—God in our everyday lives?

BEING // All people are created in God's image to reflect Him and live in relationship with Him. Sin damaged that image and brought separation, but Christians are new creations with the distinct privilege of enjoying a restored relationship with God and reflecting His character to the world in a special way.

We have the benefit of serving a God who is not located behind the walls of a building or encased in statues that we have to pray to; He is all around us. He's everywhere we go. He's dwells within us. What's more, He's ready and able to save anyone—at any time and in any place—who calls on His name. We have the deep honor and pleasure of living with the kind of hope that our God is the God who saves, and He is not thrown for a loop by anything that could ever happen to us. Be strengthened and encouraged by the fact that your God is stronger than anything you will ever face.

DOING // Because we are created to reflect God and live in relationship with Him, we should continually pursue God in His Word and through prayer, live in continual fellowship within the church, and help people who do not know Him find Him so they can live in fellowship with Him, too.

APOLOGETIC // Many today believe there are many gods and many ways to heaven, and that we are free to define God according to our personal perspectives. However, Scripture teaches there is one God (Deut. 6:4).

CHRIST

Paul wrote of Jesus in Colossians 1:15-17, "He is the image of the invisible God, the firstborn over all creation. For everything was created by Him, in heaven and on earth, the visible and the invisible, whether thrones or dominions or rulers or authorities—all things have been created through him and for him. He is before all things, and by him all things hold together." What he is describing is a God who is completely sovereign—He has complete control over everything, even the things we don't (and won't ever) know about. If we are trying to live our lives apart from His power, we won't get very far and we'll end up being broken, frustrated, and exhausted. But by submitting to His power and acting for His glory under His authority, we can become "more than conquerors" (Rom. 8:37).

What are things you try to do under your own power that you should turn over to Jesus?

COMMUNITY

When Christ ascended to Heaven, He tasked His followers to be His hands and feet on earth. If you think about it, that makes the things the church does an expression of His power. Paul told the church in Corinth, "you are the body of Christ, and individual members of it" (1 Cor. 12:27). He then goes on to list a few ways people play their different roles: some teach, some heal, some help, some administrate. The number of ways we can serve the body so that it can carry out the task God has given it are almost endless.

In what ways has God gifted you to serve your local body of believers?

How do you think you can use that to help them be Jesus' body?

CULTURE

As the church works together to be Christ's body—an extension of His unlimited power—the impact they have on the world around them will be unbelievable. There are groups not motivated by the gospel who do a lot of good for the world around them, but Christ's body should be different. The work we do should make those around us who don't believe wonder how it could be possible at all.

What kind of impact do you think the church has in the world right now?

How do you think we could work together to make that impact something people look at and say, "only God could have done this"?

Session 6

DEVOTIONS

THE PATIENCE OF GOD

God is all-powerful, timeless, sovereign, kind, good, and forgiving. We should all be so grateful for the patience of God. We have all messed up repeatedly and if God had no mercy at all, none of us would be saved.

However, we have this Bible and it shows us clearly how God is gracious toward us and wants people to be saved. This attribute of God's means a great deal to us all because of our own attributes of sinfulness.

> *The Lord does not delay his promise, as some understand delay, but is patient with you, not wanting any to perish but all to come to repentance.*
> **2 PETER 3:9**

We have failed Him so many times and we all have long lists of sins that condemn us, but God is gracious and forgiving. He is patient with us and this attribute of God's calls for gratitude on our parts. Have you ever truly considered the graciousness of God?

Describe yourself. As you do, be honest.

Now, reading over your description of yourself, did you account for the grace of God on your life?

THE FAITHFULNESS OF GOD

We are quite ridiculously privileged. As saved sinners, we are privileged because we should have been destined toward hell, but are destined toward heaven instead. However, our privilege as Christians goes beyond this. It is easy for us, having been born in this century, to overlook the deep roots of our salvation.

The gospel runs deep. Its foundations are in the very first book of the Bible. God made a promise to a man named Abraham and we are saved today because of it. Take a look at one of the many times God shared this promise to Abraham in Genesis. This particular proclamation came right after Abraham proved his dedication to God by not withholding his son Isaac:

Then the angel of the LORD called to Abraham a second time from heaven and said, "By myself I have sworn," this is the LORD's declaration: "Because you have done this thing and have not withheld your only son, I will indeed bless you and make your offspring as numerous as the stars of the sky and the sand on the seashore. Your offspring will possess the city gates of their enemies. And all the nations of the earth will be blessed by your offspring because you have obeyed my command."
GENESIS 22:15-18

Write out a prayer of thankfulness to God for His faithfulness.

In your own words, thank God for the ways in which you share in this promise made to Abraham.

THE LOVE OF GOD

God promised the nation of Israel, His own people, He would never revoke His covenant with them. Take a look at these words spoken through the prophet Isaiah:

> *Though the mountains move and the hills shake, my love will not be removed from you and my covenant of peace will not be shaken," says your compassionate LORD.*
> **ISAIAH 54:10**

Did you see the word "love" in that passage? That is an important part of this promise. It is not as though God merely signed a contract and is bound to it. Rather, He genuinely loves His people and we as New Testament believers are a part of that.

Consider the scope of this promise for a moment. God's promise to love His people is bigger than the mountains and hills. Have you ever seen a mountain? It has nothing on the promises of God. And it's important to note Isaiah also described God as compassionate.

As we study the promises of God, let it not be lost on us that God is under no obligation whatsoever to make promises to us. We are sinners, but He is perfect. He is so incredibly good. We do not deserve and are not rightfully entitled to any kind of covenant with God. Nonetheless, He has made this steadfast covenant with His people.

Express to God your gratitude for His promises.

Share with Him your thankfulness for making this covenant of which you are a member if you've trusted in Christ.

7

THE PROMISE KEEPING GOD

ENGAGE

LEVELS OF BIBLICAL LEARNING STATEMENT

God relates to His people according to His covenant promises, and even though we aren't always faithful to Him, God keeps His promises and always has and always will be faithful to us.

As a citizen of the United States, you've entered into a contract probably without even realizing it. Several, as a matter of fact. You've agreed to abide by the laws of the land, and in return, you get to have access to the different perks of being a citizen.

For instance, if you obey the rules of the road, you get to keep the privilege of driving on them. By being a citizen, you have entered into an agreement with the lawmakers that says, "If I keep up my end of the bargain by not breaking the rules, you need to keep up your end of the bargain to protect my freedom as a citizen."

On the other hand, if you don't hold up your end of the bargain, there are going to be consequences. Sometimes the consequence is that you have to go to jail. Sometimes it means you can't drive your car anymore. Sometimes it means you lose your right to vote for the people who govern you. It all depends on the terms of the conditions you've agreed to by being a United States citizen.

What do you think some of the benefits of being a citizen of a country are, rather than just vacationing there?

God deals with His people in a similar way, except His contracts are extreme. He calls them covenants.

THE COVENANT KEEPING GOD

God relates to His people according to His covenant promises, and even though we aren't always faithful to Him, God keeps His promises. He always has and always will be faithful to us.

When has someone made a promise to you and kept it? How did that affect you?

When has someone made a promise to you and broken it? How did that affect you?

When someone tells you their word is their bond, they are essentially telling you they are shackled to their promise. They couldn't escape it even if they tried. As humans, our word is not always very binding at all because we're imperfect. But God is completely different. In fact, one of the key ways God relates to His people is through promises.

What's a promise you've made to someone before?

Do you usually believe people when they promise you something? Why or why not?

When God makes a promise, He will not break it. But to help us understand just how seriously He takes His promises, He does it in a special way. Through what's called a covenant. Let's read what a covenant with God looks like. Here, God tells Abram—then a really old man without any children—he would be the father of a nation and his offspring would have lots of land. Abram asked how he'd know this was true. Look what God did.

> *He said to him, "Bring me a three-year-old cow, a three-year-old female goat, a three-year-old ram, a turtledove, and a young pigeon." So he brought all these to him, cut them in half, and laid the pieces opposite each other, but he did not cut the birds in half. Birds of prey came down on the carcasses, but Abram drove them away. As the sun was setting, a deep sleep came over Abram, and suddenly great terror and darkness descended on him. When the sun had set and it was dark, a smoking fire pot and a flaming torch appeared and passed between the divided animals. On that day the LORD made a covenant with Abram.*
> **GENESIS 15:9-12, 17-18a**

SACRIFICE AND COVENANT

Abram had to do some pretty grueling work before this covenant could be made: He had to wrangle a bunch of animals, then he had to chop them in half and arrange them exactly the way God instructed him.

Abram wouldn't have been completely unfamiliar with this process—serious as it was. It was a relatively common practice back then to make promises this way. When two people wanted to seal a deal with each other and really give their word, they'd do something like what Abram did in that passage. Then, they'd walk between the halved carcasses, through the blood, and essentially say to each other, "May what was done to these animals be done to me if I do not keep this covenant." In other words, walking through the pieces was like saying, "If I break my end of the agreement, let me be killed."

Abram was probably feeling the pressure. He was about to enter into a covenant with God—one that required both parties to be perfectly righteous.

> **Abram probably felt a little in over his head at this point. When have you felt like you were in over your head? How did it play out?**

Well, if he were feeling in over his head, it didn't last too long—because soon a deep sleep came over him. This sleep accompanied by "great terror and darkness" (Gen. 15:12) was usually a Hebrew expression for death. But here, rather than tell us Abram died, it is simply explaining that what came next was completely out of Abram's control. Because once night fell, God used two items that have symbolized Him throughout Scripture—smoke and fire—to walk down the center of the trench Himself.

Don't miss this: by having these three elements—Abram's deep sleep, the smoking pot, and the burning fire—come together, God was showing that He alone was going to be the One upholding this agreement. Abram never walked down the trench with God. God was the only perfect One, the only One worthy of making such a promise. And soon, God's promise came true. Abram had a son who became the father of the nation of Israel: God's chosen people.

Later, God would give commandments to this nation, laws they were supposed to live by. But get this: Even though nobody would or could keep the law, God never went back on His promise. His people were His people no matter what.

> **God was going to keep His promise even if Abram couldn't hold up his end of the bargain. How does that make you feel about God?**

COVENANT AND GRACE

After a few thousand years—after God's promises continued coming true for the nation of Israel—the most amazing promise came true: God's Messiah came into the world. He said a new covenant we still fit under today.

> *In the same way he also took the cup after supper and said, "This cup is the new covenant in my blood, which is poured out for you."*
> **LUKE 22:20**

Jesus used a cup of wine to illustrate this covenant, but the very next day He'd make it extremely real. He would take the place of the sacrificed animal. We didn't have to wrangle and sacrifice animals, we didn't have to spill the blood into a trench, we didn't have to walk through it. Jesus, who was God in the flesh, did this all for us.

This new covenant was initiated by God, the blood was provided by God, and the terms for it were upheld by God. The only thing we need to do in order to be a part of this new covenant and be part of God's kingdom is to put our faith in Jesus. We tell God we understand our portion of the "bargain" was covered by Christ at the Cross and trust that we are forgiven through His sacrifice on our behalf.

And this new covenant has even better news for us, because it is accompanied not by law, but by Grace (Rom. 6:14-15). We have a perfect mediator—Jesus. We have a perfect sacrifice on our behalf—Jesus. And all we have to do to enter this covenant kingdom is put our faith in Him.

If that isn't the deal of a lifetime, I don't know what is.

How does it make you feel to know God will always keep His promises to His people, even when we're imperfect?

What are some ways you can express your gratitude to God for showing us grace even though we don't deserve it?

BEING // All people are created in God's image to reflect Him and live in relationship with Him. Sin damaged that image and brought separation, but Christians are new creations with the distinct privilege of enjoying a restored relationship with God and reflecting His character to the world in a special way.

DOING // Because we are created to reflect God and live in relationship with Him, we should continually pursue God in His Word and through prayer, live in continual fellowship within the church, and help people who do not know Him find Him so they can live in fellowship with Him, too.

APOLOGETIC // Many today believe there are many gods and many ways to heaven, and that we are free to define God according to our personal perspectives. However, Scripture teaches there is one God (Deut. 6:4).

When God speaks, He speaks to and through His people—those who believe He sent His Son to die on our behalf. There is an extremely specific means of entry into His kingdom, and it is through Jesus. Jesus actually used the metaphor of a vine to illustrate this: You're either connected to God's vine or you aren't and the only way to find the kind of life that God gives is through Him (John 14:6). If someone tries to tell you there are many paths to God, that would make Jesus a liar, and He cannot lie.

CHRIST

When God promises something, He follows through. When Christ tells us He is going but will return, we can take Him at His word. But what about you—when you say something, are you trustworthy to keep your word? Christ was careful to speak only the truth. In fact, He said He came to earth so He could "testify to the truth" (John 18:37). Especially if people are watching us closely to see if we really behave like Jesus, we should take extra care to guard the words that come out of our mouths, so they resemble Christ in every way.

Would you consider yourself trustworthy? Why or why not?

How can you mold your speech so it more closely resembles Christ's?

COMMUNITY

God is the ultimate example of faithfulness to His people. Even when they repeatedly failed Him, He loved them and took them back. We have the opportunity to do that with each other, too. You're going to disappoint and upset your brother or sister in Christ, just like they're going to disappoint and upset you. That is why we must be slow to anger, quick to ask for forgiveness, and quick to forgive. God has been with us, so we should be with the people in our lives, also.

How has God shown you faithfulness?

Do you have a broken relationship with a brother or sister in the faith right now? Is there something you can do to take steps toward fixing it—either apologizing or extending forgiveness?

CULTURE

If you look at promises God made in the Old Testament, the overwhelming majority of them were made to a specific group of people: the Israelites. They were God's people, and He was their God. With only a few exceptions, His promises were for the group as a whole—not even just the people hearing the promise. They knew that they were part of a bigger story than just the one they were experience there in that moment.

For instance, when God told Israel, "'For I know the plans I have for you'—this is the LORD's declaration—'plans for your well-being, not for disaster, to give you a future and a hope,'" (Jer. 29:11) He spoke it to people in captivity. They were slaves. And those who heard it didn't even get to experience this God's promises are for His people as a whole—those who were alive thousands of years ago, those who are alive now, and those who will be alive in years to come.

Fortunately, "God's people" is not a "closed" group. God actually flung the doors wide open when He sent Jesus to die for us. Anybody can be grafted into the vine of God's people if they come through the door God sent: His Son, Jesus.

"I have a desire to see people brought into God's family." Does this statement feel like something you could say about yourself? Why or why not?

Session 7

DEVOTIONS

THE PROMISE OF REDEMPTION

Have you ever read the final words of the Bible? The final chapter of Revelation includes this striking promise from God:

> Then he showed me the river of the water of life, clear as crystal, flowing from the throne of God and of the Lamb down the middle of the city's main street. The tree of life was on each side of the river, bearing twelve kinds of fruit, producing its fruit every month. The leaves of the tree are for healing the nations, and there will no longer be any curse. The throne of God and of the Lamb will be in the city, and his servants will worship him. They will see his face, and his name will be on their foreheads. Night will be no more; people will not need the light of a lamp or the light of the sun, because the Lord God will give them light, and they will reign forever and ever.
> **REVELATION 22:1-5**

As you stay tuned in to what is happening on the world's stage, you likely see that we need this healing. We need healing among the nations. Only God could bring about this kind of peace we need and He has said He will do it. It is written in His Bible! So, He is accountable to it.

Think about this for a minute: He could have gotten by without promising this, but He made the promise anyway. He could have left us in our turmoil forever, but He has instead promised to redeem. The night must end. The sun will rise. The very source of light for heaven itself is the direct presence of our God and we have this promise in writing!

Share with God how your heart feels when you consider God's promise to fully and finally redeem you?.

Journal how this affects your view of life itself, knowing that one sweet day, we will be with God forever.

HE WILL RETURN

Look at this brilliant thing God has done. He has prophesied His return, but strategically left us wondering about its timing. Because He will return like a thief in the night, we have to live our lives as though His return is tomorrow because it very well could be. If He had announced a specific date, we would abuse that knowledge by living sinfully until the day before that date, but instead He makes this promise:

> Then he said to me, "These words are faithful and true. The Lord, the God of the spirits of the prophets, has sent his angel to show his servants what must soon take place."
> "Look, I am coming soon! Blessed is the one who keeps the words of the prophecy of this book."
> **REVELATION 22:6-7**

These words were written in the first century and they become truer every day. It is always accurate to say His return is "soon." In fact, the second time you say it is more accurate than the first time you say it. He has promised not to abandon us in this mess and leave the world the broken way that it is. Soon, He will make right every last thing that is wrong. Every single issue in the world will one day be resolved. He has not forgotten us. He will come back. So, we can rest in that hope.

Let your anxieties fall to the side. Express to God your sense of relief knowing He has promised to return.

Then, commit to God that you will realign your priorities in light of His promise to come back.

OUR GOD IS WITH US

How incredibly comforting it is to know our God is with us. He is present among His people and is faithful to us. This means you! Absolutely no matter what happens among your friends, no matter what happens in your family, God will always be there for you.

In the Old Testament, God made a promise to His people and that promise applies today.

> *"Be strong and courageous; don't be terrified or afraid of them. For the LORD your God is the one who will go with you; he will not leave you or abandon you."*
> **DEUTERONOMY 31:6**

Really and truly, do you believe this? When you look at your life from the outside, do you see yourself as all alone? You are not. God is with you. He will positively always be with you. There is nowhere you could go that He is not already there. There is nothing you could do to reduce His love for you. There is nothing you can do about His presence. He will not back out of the deal even when you mess up. He will not change His mind about you; it is made up already. You cannot and will not scare Him off; even when you are at your very worst. He quite simply will never leave you or forsake you.

God has promised He will not leave you. How does that make you feel? How should you respond to this truth?

Express to God your thankfulness to Him. Journal here a prayer of thanksgiving to your perfectly faithful God.

GOD IS RIGHTEOUS

ENGAGE

LEVELS OF BIBLICAL LEARNING STATEMENT
God is loving and righteous, grieves the impact of sin on the world, and will one day make right all that sin has damaged.

A 1993 article in the Los Angeles Times tells the story of Mike Decalvo, who was a runner competing in a collegiate cross-country championship. When the runners reached an embankment on their route, only five of them stayed true to the course. When Mike and the four other runners rejoined the pack, they were way behind. He ended up finishing in as number 123.

This is the interesting part: Mike and the four other runners were the only ones who actually followed the rules. The others had reduced their distance by about 1,000 meters. To Mike's disappointment, the race officials did not overturn the results. This is what he had to say about it: "I'm upset, … If I had stayed on the wrong course, I would have finished respectably. But when you read the official results, I'm 123 out of 128 runners."[1]

In this example, Mike and the four who ran with him were the obedient ones. You might even say they behaved righteously: They didn't break the rules they were supposed to follow.

How does it make you feel when people are treated unfairly? What's an example of this from your life?

Unlike the judges in that race, God is a Judge who expects righteousness and punishes unrighteousness, but we have done a pretty good job of veering off course. Thankfully, God has made a way for us to get back on course, and is actively working to restore the world from the impact of our sin.

GOD OF RIGHTEOUSNESS

You are no stranger to rules. They're everywhere you go from the moment you wake up until you go to sleep at night. There are rules in your house, rules on the road, rules at school and in stores and in public life. You had no say in what these rules would be; they were put there by someone in authority over you—anyone from your parents to the country's lawmakers.

The system we have in place to make sure everything is in accordance with the rules is called justice. Justice allows us to punish people who break the rules and ensures the freedom of those who keep them. But our justice is based on something we've made. The rules of our homes, our schools, our country.

There may be some rules you think are unfair. But what are some rules (or laws) you think are very fair?

Why do you think it's important to have rules in place at all?

God's justice is entirely different. He didn't have someone above Him who gave Him a standard to live by. Instead, He is the standard to live by. Because God aligns perfectly with His standard of perfection, we call Him righteous. David put it like this:

The LORD is righteous in all his ways and faithful in all his acts.
PSALM 145:17

This is good news for us. This means God is not going to surprise us in the way He deals with us—His creation. He is always going to act in a way that aligns with His standard. He will not suddenly turn into a god of evil and chaos because it is simply not in His nature. No matter what He does, it will always be righteous. He will always be a God of His word. He will always act the way He has said He will act.

GOD OF JUSTICE

But part of this just, righteous action means that He stands against those who are not righteous, those who place their own desires above His own. Because He is a just God, He must punish sin. And He absolutely will.

> *The righteous LORD is in her; he does no wrong. He applies his justice morning by morning; he does not fail at dawn.*
> **ZEPHANIAH 3:5**

These sound amazing! They speak of a God who is stable and righteous and just and never-failing. But the problem is that they come in the middle of verses describing the wickedness of a rebellious, blasphemous city.

> *Woe to the city that is rebellious and defiled, the oppressive city! She has not obeyed; she has not accepted discipline. She has not trusted in the Lord; she has not drawn near to her God. The princes within her are roaring lions; her judges are wolves of the night, which leave nothing for the morning. Her prophets are reckless—treacherous men. Her priests profane the sanctuary; they do violence to instruction.*
> **ZEPHANIAH 3:1-4**

Looking at verse 5 in order here, God seems a little menacing. Like a challenger. He's the unchanging standard, standing above a city that has forsaken Him. Because He is righteous, He has every right to be angry when His people turn away from Him.

What do you think it looks like to turn away from God?

What kind of reaction do you think is right for God to have when we do that?

But remember: God is just. God is righteous. God is not going to do something against His nature. This is encouraging, because while He is just and righteous, He is also loving.

GOD OF LOVE

Do you remember in the Garden of Eden, right after Adam and Eve sinned, then covered up their sin, then shifted blame all over the place to avoid getting in trouble? God was right to cast them out of the Garden. But look at what He did:

> The LORD God made clothing from skins for the man and his wife, and he clothed them.
> **GENESIS 3:21**

They had just deliberately disobeyed Him, but He still provided for them—and did so at a cost. Where do you think He got those skins? They probably came from an animal. Another piece of His creation. He sacrificed something He made to provide for these people who had just rebelled against Him. They'd broken His heart, but still He gave.

If you read the Bible cover to cover, you will see this trend over and over and over again. God's people will sin against Him at every turn, and still He takes them back. There is an entire book about God's relationship with His people, written by Hosea. In that book, Hosea represented God, and Hosea's wife represented Israel, God's chosen people. Over and over, Hosea's wife runs away and cheats on Him, and every time, Hosea went to where she was, saved her from difficult situations, and welcomed her back into His home.

Because God is just, sin must be punished. But because God is loving, He provided a way for us to be free from that punishment. Paul put it this way:

> But God proves his own love for us in that while we were still sinners, Christ died for us.
> **ROMANS 5:8**

While we were still sinners, Christ died for us. God didn't wait for us to get our act together and come back on our own; He relentlessly pursued us even while we were neck-deep in filth. And He gave His only Son—He gave Himself—to take the punishment we deserved.

When has someone wronged you? How did you handle that situation?

What may be most miraculous of all is that God is working all things so to make right everything sin has damaged. All of the havoc sin wreaked on our world will be corrected. All of the bitterness it has put into our hearts will be soothed. All of the rebellion in our spirit will be squashed, and we will live together with Him in perfect harmony.

Our God promises us a good and just future free from all the havoc and destruction sin has brought into our world. (See Rev. 21:1-4.) A future free from sorrow, pain, and death. Because God is just, righteous, and loving, He will not stop working in us until our home is with Him.

BEING // All people are created in God's image to reflect Him and live in relationship with Him. Sin damaged that image and brought separation, but Christians are new creations with the distinct privilege of enjoying a restored relationship with God and reflecting His character to the world in a special way.

When Christ died, He gave you an option. You can accept His sacrifice on your behalf and follow Him, or you can reject it. Once you accept it, a miracle occurs. His righteousness gets applied to you. Then, whenever God looks at your life and sees Christ crucified on your behalf, He sees you the same way He sees His Son: spotless, blameless, and righteous. If you have been made righteous by Christ's sacrifice, take a moment to understand just how heavy that is, and then from the overflow of your gratitude for His sacrifice, live a life that is pleasing to God.

DOING // Because we are created to reflect God and live in relationship with Him, we should continually pursue God in His Word and through prayer, live in continual fellowship within the church, and help people who do not know Him find Him so they can live in fellowship with Him, too.

APOLOGETIC // Many today believe there are many gods and many ways to heaven, and that we are free to define God according to our personal perspectives. However, Scripture teaches there is one God (Deut. 6:4).

CHRIST

When some Pharisees brought a woman caught in adultery to Jesus, they wanted to see what He'd do. According to the law, they had every right to stone her—to kill her for the damage that had been done both to her family and the family of the man she committed adultery with. That's why what He said was so surprising: "The one without sin among you should be the first to throw a stone at her" (John 8:7).

Even though she deserved the punishment of death, Jesus offered her forgiveness. And He offers the exact same thing to you.

When did you accept Jesus' sacrifice on your behalf? How did that change you? How has it affected you since?

COMMUNITY

God is a God of restoration. He has quite the knack for it, and He loves to see His children restored. Sometimes we can tend to not love it as much as He does. If someone wrongs us, we want to see justice done. We want people to pay for what they did. As God's people, we should look at those among us who have failed with compassion and the desire to see them restored. None of us innocent, so we should extend restoration and forgiveness to those among us who have fallen away, as well.

What do you think it means to be "restored"?

How do you think we go about restoring someone who has messed up? Can you think of a situation where someone shouldn't be restored? Explain.

CULTURE

God hates sin. He hates it. But at the same time, He gave up His Son to die on our behalf while we were still sinners. As we interact more and more with those around us, we will find that many are living lives in no way bring God glory. But remember before you start casting stones at them that you have been exactly where they were at one time. As Christians, we should be vocal about what is sin and what isn't. At the same time, we should be even more vocal about the One who saves us from it.

How do you think we balance between "hating sin" and "loving the sinner"?

Session 8

DEVOTIONS

MAKE DISCIPLES

Our existence is not by chance. It is purposeful.

We have a mission for our restless hearts and it is divine. Jesus gave the Great Commission to His disciples in the Book of Matthew. This is simultaneously a set of marching orders and a promise from God. The Great Commission is the call for Christians to make disciples. Look closely. Do you see the promise built into it?

> *"Truly I tell you, whatever you bind on earth will have been bound in heaven, and whatever you loose on earth will have been loosed in heaven. Again, truly I tell you, if two of you on earth agree about any matter that you pray for, it will be done for you by my Father in heaven. For where two or three are gathered together in my name, I am there among them."*
> **MATTHEW 18:18-20**

So, just on the heels of this commissioning comes the promise to be with us always. Even if the entire world goes crazy, He will be with us. Even when tragedy strikes, He will be with us through it. His promise is irrevocable, and He will always follow-through. Revel in this promise and obey this commissioning. See the truth of the promise as you reach out to people with the gospel of Jesus Christ and walk with those people through their next steps in the faith, from belief to baptism to serving in church to using their spiritual gifts to going on mission. Make disciples and experience this nearness of God.

List the names of people you can engage with the gospel.

What are your own next steps in the faith? Remember Jesus promised to be with us always, even to the end of the age.

JUST AND JUSTIFIER

For all have sinned and fall short of the glory of God. They are justified freely by his grace through the redemption that is in Christ Jesus.
ROMANS 3:23-24

Most believers will be familiar with verse 23, but verse 24 is often overlooked. We frequently see Romans 3:23 used to teach about our sin nature and rightfully so. It points out that every one of us has sinned and fallen short. We inherited this nature from Adam and Eve. Think about it: If we were in the same position in the Garden of Eden, then we all would have disobeyed as well.

So, it is right to point this out with Romans 3:23, but the thought is not complete in this one verse. We have to look at the next one, which contains God's promise that we sinners may be justified.

Though our sins are like scarlet, we are made white as snow. Though we have failed over and over, we sinners are made righteous by the work of Jesus. This is the best news you'll hear today—that we sinners are proclaimed righteous and justified before the Judge is no small feat on God's part. Look at what God has done. He made a way for us to be with Him without compromising at all in His holiness.

Because of our sin, what do we actually deserve?

Instead of getting what we deserve, what does God give us through justification?

ETERNAL LIFE

Jesus, in meeting with Nicodemus at night, made a statement that has become the most famous verse in the Bible. Take a look:

For God loved the world in this way: He gave his one and only Son, so that everyone who believes in him will not perish but have eternal life.
JOHN 3:16

In its original context, this verse was actually spoken one-on-one in a private conversation with a Pharisee. It may be overly familiar at this point, but revisit it anyway. There is a promise from God in it. Sift carefully through the words once more, reading it as though you were reading it for the very first time.

This particular promise from God should mean a great deal to us as mortals. Death is the all-eclipsing thing to us. The greatest pain we feel in this life is when we grieve the death of someone we love. However, Jesus overwhelmed death. Jesus' resurrection secured our victory over the grave. Now, if we believe fully in Jesus, we will not be defeated by death! Instead, we can have eternal life.

This is how it was meant to be. We can put this verse on like a warm coat and our souls will say, "Yes, this is what I was made for." We were made for life and God promises us exactly that if we believe in Jesus. You were meant for an eternal life. Are you living it?

What are some social media channels you could use to proclaim this gospel?

Journal a commitment to God that you will spread the good news of this eternal, never-ending, everlasting life as Jesus promised.

ENGAGE

Start the session by reading the *Levels of Biblical Learning Statement* on page 6. Then, use the introduction provided as a way to begin your group time before transitioning to the Discuss section.

DISCUSS

Be sure to read the Discuss section on pages 7-9 before coming together as a group. Doing so will allow you to be familiar with the material and will help you select which portions of the material you would like to cover in the allotted amount of group time. Look for places in the Discuss section where you can add a personal anecdote to a question or a Scripture passage to share in addition to what has been provided. Making preparations like these will help your group time run more smoothly and be more effective in the end.

LIVE IT OUT

After your group works through the Discuss section, take some time to move through the application found in the Live It Out section on pages 10-11. Look for specific, personal ways you can connect with the material from your own past. Sharing a personal story or illustration that connects with the lesson is a great way to connect with students and creates an atmosphere where students also feel comfortable sharing.

WEEKLY LEADER TIPS

- Introduce the personal devotions that follow Session 1, and remind students to complete the session devotions on pages 12-15 before your next meeting.
- Challenge students to memorize the Levels of Biblical Learning Statement for Session 1.
- Encourage students to be in the habit of building into their personal prayer lives with what they have learned this week.

WEEKLY LEADER NOTES

....

....

....

....

ENGAGE

Start the session by reading the *Levels of Biblical Learning Statement* on page 16. Then, use the introduction provided as a way to begin your group time before transitioning to the Discuss section.

DISCUSS

Be sure to read the Discuss section on pages 17-19 before coming together as a group. Doing so will allow you to be familiar with the material and will help you select which portions of the material you would like to cover in the allotted amount of group time. Look for places in the Discuss section where you can add a personal anecdote to a question or a Scripture passage to share in addition to what has been provided. Making preparations like these will help your group time run more smoothly and be more effective in the end.

LIVE IT OUT

After your group works through the Discuss section, take some time to move through the application found in the Live It Out section on pages 20-21. Look for specific, personal ways you can connect with the material from your own past. Sharing a personal story or illustration that connects with the lesson is a great way to connect with students and creates an atmosphere where students also feel comfortable sharing.

WEEKLY LEADER TIPS

- Introduce the personal devotions that follow Session 2, and remind students to complete the session devotions on pages 22-25 before your next meeting.
- Challenge students to memorize the Levels of Biblical Learning Statement for Session 2.
- Encourage students to be in the habit of building into their personal prayer lives with what they have learned this week.

WEEKLY LEADER NOTES

....

....

....

....

ENGAGE

Start the session by reading the *Levels of Biblical Learning Statement* on page 26. Then, use the introduction provided as a way to begin your group time before transitioning to the Discuss section.

DISCUSS

Be sure to read the Discuss section on pages 27-29 before coming together as a group. Doing so will allow you to be familiar with the material and will help you select which portions of the material you would like to cover in the allotted amount of group time. Look for places in the Discuss section where you can add a personal anecdote to a question or a Scripture passage to share in addition to what has been provided. Making preparations like these will help your group time run more smoothly and be more effective in the end.

LIVE IT OUT

After your group works through the Discuss section, take some time to move through the application found in the Live It Out section on pages 30-31. Look for specific, personal ways you can connect with the material from your own past. Sharing a personal story or illustration that connects with the lesson is a great way to connect with students and creates an atmosphere where students also feel comfortable sharing.

WEEKLY LEADER TIPS

- Introduce the personal devotions that follow Session 3, and remind students to complete the session devotions on pages 32-35 before your next meeting.
- Challenge students to memorize the Levels of Biblical Learning Statement for Session 3.
- Encourage students to be in the habit of building into their personal prayer lives with what they have learned this week.

WEEKLY LEADER NOTES

....

....

....

....

ENGAGE

Start the session by reading the *Levels of Biblical Learning Statement* on page 36. Then, use the introduction provided as a way to begin your group time before transitioning to the Discuss section.

DISCUSS

Be sure to read the Discuss section on pages 37-39 before coming together as a group. Doing so will allow you to be familiar with the material and will help you select which portions of the material you would like to cover in the allotted amount of group time. Look for places in the Discuss section where you can add a personal anecdote to a question or a Scripture passage to share in addition to what has been provided. Making preparations like these will help your group time run more smoothly and be more effective in the end.

LIVE IT OUT

After your group works through the Discuss section, take some time to move through the application found in the Live It Out section on pages 40-41. Look for specific, personal ways you can connect with the material from your own past. Sharing a personal story or illustration that connects with the lesson is a great way to connect with students and creates an atmosphere where students also feel comfortable sharing.

WEEKLY LEADER TIPS

- Introduce the personal devotions that follow Session 4, and remind students to complete the session devotions on pages 42-45 before your next meeting.
- Challenge students to memorize the Levels of Biblical Learning Statement for Session 4.
- Encourage students to be in the habit of building into their personal prayer lives with what they have learned this week.

WEEKLY LEADER NOTES

....

....

....

....

ENGAGE

Start the session by reading the *Levels of Biblical Learning Statement* on page 46. Then, use the introduction provided as a way to begin your group time before transitioning to the Discuss section.

DISCUSS

Be sure to read the Discuss section on pages 47-49 before coming together as a group. Doing so will allow you to be familiar with the material and will help you select which portions of the material you would like to cover in the allotted amount of group time. Look for places in the Discuss section where you can add a personal anecdote to a question or a Scripture passage to share in addition to what has been provided. Making preparations like these will help your group time run more smoothly and be more effective in the end.

LIVE IT OUT

After your group works through the Discuss section, take some time to move through the application found in the Live It Out section on pages 50-51. Look for specific, personal ways you can connect with the material from your own past. Sharing a personal story or illustration that connects with the lesson is a great way to connect with students and creates an atmosphere where students also feel comfortable sharing.

WEEKLY LEADER TIPS

- Introduce the personal devotions that follow Session 5, and remind students to complete the session devotions on pages 52-55 before your next meeting.
- Challenge students to memorize the Levels of Biblical Learning Statement for Session 5.
- Encourage students to be in the habit of building into their personal prayer lives with what they have learned this week.

WEEKLY LEADER NOTES

....

....

....

....

ENGAGE

Start the session by reading the *Levels of Biblical Learning Statement* on page 56. Then, use the introduction provided as a way to begin your group time before transitioning to the Discuss section.

DISCUSS

Be sure to read the Discuss section on pages 57-59 before coming together as a group. Doing so will allow you to be familiar with the material and will help you select which portions of the material you would like to cover in the allotted amount of group time. Look for places in the Discuss section where you can add a personal anecdote to a question or a Scripture passage to share in addition to what has been provided. Making preparations like these will help your group time run more smoothly and be more effective in the end.

LIVE IT OUT

After your group works through the Discuss section, take some time to move through the application found in the Live It Out section on pages 60-61. Look for specific, personal ways you can connect with the material from your own past. Sharing a personal story or illustration that connects with the lesson is a great way to connect with students and creates an atmosphere where students also feel comfortable sharing.

WEEKLY LEADER TIPS

- Introduce the personal devotions that follow Session 6, and remind students to complete the session devotions on pages 62-65 before your next meeting.
- Challenge students to memorize the Levels of Biblical Learning Statement for Session 6.
- Encourage students to be in the habit of building into their personal prayer lives with what they have learned this week.

WEEKLY LEADER NOTES

....

....

....

....

ENGAGE

Start the session by reading the *Levels of Biblical Learning Statement* on page 66. Then, use the introduction provided as a way to begin your group time before transitioning to the Discuss section.

DISCUSS

Be sure to read the Discuss section on pages 67-69 before coming together as a group. Doing so will allow you to be familiar with the material and will help you select which portions of the material you would like to cover in the allotted amount of group time. Look for places in the Discuss section where you can add a personal anecdote to a question or a Scripture passage to share in addition to what has been provided. Making preparations like these will help your group time run more smoothly and be more effective in the end.

LIVE IT OUT

After your group works through the Discuss section, take some time to move through the application found in the Live It Out section on pages 70-71. Look for specific, personal ways you can connect with the material from your own past. Sharing a personal story or illustration that connects with the lesson is a great way to connect with students and creates an atmosphere where students also feel comfortable sharing.

WEEKLY LEADER TIPS

- Introduce the personal devotions that follow Session 7, and remind students to complete the session devotions on pages 72-75 before your next meeting.
- Challenge students to memorize the Levels of Biblical Learning Statement for Session 7.
- Encourage students to be in the habit of building into their personal prayer lives with what they have learned this week.

WEEKLY LEADER NOTES

....

....

....

....

ENGAGE

Start the session by reading the *Levels of Biblical Learning Statement* on page 76. Then, use the introduction provided as a way to begin your group time before transitioning to the Discuss section.

DISCUSS

Be sure to read the Discuss section on pages 77-79 before coming together as a group. Doing so will allow you to be familiar with the material and will help you select which portions of the material you would like to cover in the allotted amount of group time. Look for places in the Discuss section where you can add a personal anecdote to a question or a Scripture passage to share in addition to what has been provided. Making preparations like these will help your group time run more smoothly and be more effective in the end.

LIVE IT OUT

After your group works through the Discuss section, take some time to move through the application found in the Live It Out section on pages 80-81. Look for specific, personal ways you can connect with the material from your own past. Sharing a personal story or illustration that connects with the lesson is a great way to connect with students and creates an atmosphere where students also feel comfortable sharing.

WEEKLY LEADER TIPS

- Introduce the personal devotions that follow Session 8, and remind students to complete the session devotions on pages 82-85 before your next meeting.
- Challenge students to memorize the Levels of Biblical Learning Statement for Session 8.
- Encourage students to be in the habit of building into their personal prayer lives with what they have learned this week.

WEEKLY LEADER NOTES

....

....

....

....

SOURCES

SESSION 2

1. Cady Lang, "Keanu Reeves Was the Best Companion on a Bus Ride With a Bunch of Stranded Plane Passengers," *Time*, March 25, 2019, http://time.com/5558494/keanu-reeves-bus/.

2. Andrew T. Young, "Eye injuries of early solar observers," *San Diego State Universtiy*, 2012, https://aty.sdsu.edu/~aty/vision/others.html.

SESSION 3

1. *Tales of Ancient India*, trans. J. A. B. van Buitenen (Chicago: University of Chicago Press, 1959), 53.

2. *Merriam-Webster,* s.v. "worship," accessed May 2, 2019, https://www.merriam-webster.com/dictionary/worship.

SESSION 4

1. Calvin R. Stapert, "Johann Sebastian Bach," *Christianity Today*, accessed April 15, 2019, https://www.christianitytoday.com/history/issues/issue-95/johann-sebastian-bach-composer-german-protestant-baroque.html

2. Joshua J. Mark, "Enuma Elish - The Babylonian Epic of Creation - Full Text," *Ancient History Encyclopedia*, May 4, 2018, https://www.ancient.eu/article/225/enuma-elish---the-babylonian-epic-of-creation---fu/.

3. Donald Mackenzie, *Egyptian Myth and Legend*, (Whitefish, MT: Kessinger Publishing, LLC, 2006), 48.

4. Daniel Appel, "5 Mythological Stories About How the World Was Created," *Ultraculture*, accessed April 15, 2019, https://ultraculture.org/blog/2016/04/28/5-mythological-stories-world-created/.

SESSION 5

1. Gary Chapman, *The 5 Love Languages: The Secret to Love that Lasts* (Chicago, IL: Northfield Publishing, 2015).

SESSION 8

1. "A Race Full of Confusion: Despite Costly Wrong Turn, Cross-Country Results Stand," *Los Angeles Times*, November 24, 1993, https://www.latimes.com/archives/la-xpm-1993-11-24-sp-60318-story.html.

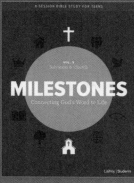

Get the most from your study.

Customize your Bible study time with a guided experience and additional resources.

People throughout the world claim to know God and what God is like. One religion says God is like this while another says He is like that. So who is right, and how can we gain genuine knowledge about God in the midst of the various opinions around us? Where can we confidently turn for answers?

In Volume 1 of *Milestones*, we explore questions like these surrounding the person, character, and mission of God as revealed in Scripture. Over the course of eight sessions, students will:

- uncover key theological truths about God.
- unpack why those truths are important.
- discover ways to engage their community and culture in light of them.

It is our hope that by going through this volume, students will grow in their personal knowledge and understanding of God and His world. We also hope God will use this study to equip another generation to boldly proclaim the truth about who He is and the message of hope He has provided through the gospel to a world that desperately needs it.

Lifeway designs trustworthy experiences that fuel ministry. Today, the ministries of Lifeway reach more than 160 countries around the globe. For specific information on Lifeway Students, visit lifeway.com/students.

ADDITIONAL RESOURCES

MILESTONES: VOL. 2, JESUS
Explore questions surrounding the person, character, and mission of Jesus in eight sessions.

MILESTONES: VOL. 1-6
Continue the series with volumes 1-6 available at www.lifeway.com/milestones